Young Jobhunter

Interview
Skills

D1390737

Young Jobhunters
Interview Skills

Helen Cooper

Young Jobhunters: Interview Skills

This first edition published by Trotman, an imprint of Crimson Publishing, Westminster House, Kew Road, Richmond, Surrey TW9 2ND

Author: Helen Cooper

© Trotman Publishing 2011

British Library Cataloguing in Publication data
A catalogue record of this book is available from the British Library

ISBN: 978-1-84455-3-853

Typeset by: Refinecatch Ltd, Bungay, Suffolk

Printed and bound by Ashford Colour Press Ltd., Gosport, Hants.

CONTENTS

ACKNOWLEDGEMENTS

This book was written with the invaluable help and support of a number of people.

My very grateful thanks therefore go to:

- Lauren – whose first interviews helped to inspire this book
- Kate – for her book-writing advice
- Mike – for sharing and supporting the book-writing experience
- Alex – for the IT support
- Chris – for everything.

GLOSSARY

Action plan This is a written plan that identifies your goals – wanting to improve your interview skills, for example. It includes setting out the steps you need to take and the timescales for achieving your objectives.

Careers adviser People who offer career advice and support call themselves a variety of different titles – careers adviser, career coach, career consultant, career professional, interview coach and so on. For simplicity this book uses the term 'careers adviser' throughout.

Human resources (HR) This is the department in a company that looks after the recruitment, training and management of staff.

Job description A company's written description of what a job is about, including the key tasks that someone will do and their responsibilities.

Induction training When a company takes on a new employee, they may offer them some special training, called induction training, when they first start work to help them learn all about the job and the organisation.

Person specification This is written by a company to describe the knowledge, skills, qualifications and work experience that someone needs to have in order to do the job.

Psychometric tests A special type of selection test used by some companies when they are recruiting staff. They can help a company to find out more about you by testing particular skills and personality types.

Transferable skills Transferable skills can be useful in a variety of different jobs and work situations. They include communication, team working, leadership and time management skills.

INTRODUCTION

Congratulations, panic stations . . . !

This is a very common way to find yourself feeling when you are invited to your first job interview.

Until now your job hunting has probably included:

- thinking about which job or career you would like to do
- checking out qualifications and training schemes
- looking through job adverts
- writing a CV and filling out application forms.

This can all take up a lot of time and not every job application is successful. So getting a telephone call or letter inviting you to an interview is great news.

However, it can also sometimes take you a bit by surprise. One moment you are in the midst of applying for jobs, then suddenly you have an actual date and time for a real interview on the calendar.

Your first interview

If this is your first ever interview, you might find yourself thinking about things like these:

- What will happen at my interview?
- Who will I meet?
- What should I wear?
- What questions will I be asked?
- How will the interviewer decide who to give the job to?

So although it is a real cause for celebration when a company invites you to an interview, it can also raise a lot of queries. And you might feel a bit anxious – or absolutely terrified!

However, there are *lots* of things you can do to really improve how well you do at your job interview. This is why I enjoy doing interview coaching with clients and why I have written this book.

If you have never had an interview before, doing some interview preparation can help you develop your interview skills. And spending time doing the *right* preparation can make a big difference to the chance of you being offered the job.

What are interviews?

So just what are interviews? They can be a short chat with one person, or involve a whole day of formal interviews and tests. Your job interview might be for a range of different types of work, for example:

- Saturday job
- work experience
- first job after school, college or university.

Or it might be your first formal interview.

Whatever type of interview you have been invited to, this book will help you to understand the interview process and how to prepare well for it.

How can interview preparation help?

I have interviewed lots of people for different jobs and there are always some who really stand out on the day. Sometimes this is for very good reasons, but it can also be for all the wrong reasons! Some common difficulties at a first interview include:

- being very anxious
- being too laid back and unprepared
- struggling to give relevant or concise answers
- not knowing enough about the job or company
- not speaking clearly
- not making enough eye contact with the interviewer
- having difficulty 'selling' yourself.

You can easily avoid or overcome any of these issues, though – just by spending some time thinking about and preparing for your interview. Even a few hours' preparation will make a huge difference and can quickly improve your interview skills.

About this book

This book will take you step by step through the interview process. It will help you understand and plan every stage before, during and after your interview.

It will enable you to:

- understand the interview process
- identify the right types of interview preparation
- plan your interview preparation
- develop your interview skills
- improve your confidence levels
- stand out from the crowd.

The book contains a range of tips, quizzes, case studies and checklists. These will help you to organise your interview preparation and practise your interview skills.

TIP Any time spent doing interview preparation is time well spent.

If you have plenty of time, you may want to read through the whole of this book. However, if your interview is just days or hours away, focus on the chapters that seem most useful for you.

To help you find your way around this book, here is a brief outline of each chapter.

- **Chapter 1 Interviews: what are they all about?**
  Explains what happens at interviews, why it is important to prepare for them and why it can be useful to think about things from the interviewer's point of view.

- **Chapter 2 Planning for success**
  Will help you to decide what interview preparation to do, how to make the best use of the time that you have and how to draw up an effective personalised plan.

- **Chapter 3 Preparation, preparation, preparation!**
  Takes you through some of the key areas of interview preparation, including a step-by-step guide to ensure that you have covered everything.

- **Chapter 4 What type of interview?**
  Describes the different types of interview that you might come across and how to handle them, including: face-to-face interviews, panel interviews, telephone interviews and group interviews.

- **Chapter 5 Selection tests and assessment centres**
  Identifies a variety of selection tests and assessment centre approaches and how to prepare for them, including: presentations, psychometric tests, case studies and in-tray exercises.

- **Chapter 6 Aim to impress**
  Explains the importance of first impressions, describes how to create a good impression and discusses the vital role of body language at interviews.

■ **Chapter 7 Standing out from the crowd**
Will help you to identify your own key strengths, how to present these in the best possible light at your interview and convince the company to offer *you* the job.

■ **Chapter 8 Facing your fears**
Explains the causes and symptoms of anxiety and describes techniques and coping strategies to help you manage your stress levels in an interview.

■ **Chapter 9 Questions, questions and more questions!**
Identifies different types of interview questions and how to answer them effectively, as well as dealing with tricky questions and offering ideas for questions that *you* can ask.

■ **Chapter 10 Top 10 interview questions**
Highlights some popular 'Top 10' interview questions, including step-by-step guides to answering them.

■ **Chapter 11 Waiting to hear . . .**
Describes ways to manage the 'waiting game' after your interview, the importance of writing up some notes afterwards and keeping your job hunting on track.

■ **Chapter 12 How to handle being offered the job, or not**
Explains what to think about if you are offered the job and how to negotiate the deal – as well as strategies for coping and moving on if you don't get the job.

■ **Chapter 13 Next time!**
This final chapter will help you to review your first interview experience and draw up an action plan for developing your interview skills for the future.

Good luck with your first interview!

1 INTERVIEWS: WHAT ARE THEY ALL ABOUT?

Being invited to your first job interview is brilliant news! All that time preparing your job application has paid off and now a real company wants to meet you. You are an important step closer to getting a job and starting your career.

However, now that you have been offered an interview, you might have lots of questions and perhaps some concerns about what lies ahead.

It is therefore very useful to consider just what interviews are all about. This will help you to understand what interviewers are looking for. It will also explain how preparing effectively for your interview will help to boost your confidence and manage your stress levels.

This chapter will:

■ describe what interviews are and why we have them
■ explain what happens at interviews
■ highlight what interviewers are looking for
■ help you identify how you feel about your interview
■ explain why it can help to prepare for your interview.

What is a job interview?

Job interviews are really a special type of meeting. And meetings are all about different people talking together.

For example, you might arrange to see friends one evening and catch up on all their news. And you might meet up at someone's house, or perhaps there is a party somewhere. Whatever the plan, you are likely to be looking forward to a night out!

So what makes job interviews so different from meeting up with friends at a party?

Well, they may in fact have some things in common. For example, most people don't go to a party or an interview every day of the week: so they are both *special events* and you might even have some similar questions about them.

- Who is going to be there?
- What am I going to wear?
- How am I going to get there?

You may therefore find yourself doing some planning and preparation for a party, just as you should for an interview. These are not everyday events and you therefore need to think ahead and make some plans.

It is also very common to find yourself feeling both excited and a bit nervous about special events. This is because you are not quite sure what lies ahead and how things will go.

So what makes interviews different?

There are some big differences between parties and interviews. For example, you might be looking forward to chatting with friends at a party and having a relaxing time, but at an interview:

- you are not likely to know anyone
- an interviewer is going to ask you lots of questions
- you will be hoping to give the interviewer all the right answers and make a good impression because they have something that you really want – **a job!**

At an interview it can feel as though it is the *interviewer* who is in control. After all, they set the date, invite you along and get to ask the questions.

And, of course, they also choose who is offered the job.

Interviews can therefore feel like a major test or exam, with you in the hot seat. If you think about them like this, it is not surprising that they can seem pretty stressful.

The good news, though, is that the right kind of preparation can help you feel more in control of the interview process. And this can help you to be more confident and clear about how to convince a company that they should be offering the job to *you*.

How are you feeling about your interview?

Interviews can make you feel excited, nervous, proud, worried, happy, terrified – and often a real mix of different emotions. Take a moment now to think how you are feeling about your interview:

What are you looking forward to about your interview?
What concerns do you have about your interview?

If you have a longer list of concerns than things you are looking forward to, that is quite normal. So one of the key aims of this book is to help you to think about your first interview in a positive way.

To begin this process it can be helpful to understand why we have interviews and to consider things from the interviewer's perspective.

Why do we have job interviews?

Companies organise interviews to try to find the best person to do a job. Interviews are often only one stage in a recruitment process that may take a number of weeks, or even months. This is because finding the right person can be complicated and take time to get right.

Job recruitment process

Job vacancy arises
Job description and person specification prepared
Job advertised
Company receives applications
Company selects interview candidates
Interviews/selection tests held
Company decides who to appoint
References checked
Appointment letter sent

When a company has a job vacancy, they want to find someone with the right skills and qualifications. These can vary a lot, depending on the job; so the first thing a company has to do is think about the type of person they need. They may write a short list, or draw up more detailed and formal lists.

These can include:

- job description – to explain what the job is about and the key tasks
- person specification – the knowledge, skills, qualifications and work experience that someone needs to have in order to do the job.

Smaller companies may not have much written information about a job, but larger organisations often write very detailed job descriptions and person specifications.

The company will then advertise the job, for example via a newspaper, company website or recruitment agency. A job advert will highlight important information about the type of work and the person needed to do it.

You therefore need to make sure that your CV or application form covers as many points as possible from a job advert, job description or person specification. This can really increase your chance of being asked to an interview.

If you have been offered an interview, you have therefore already convinced a company that you are one of the best applicants!

TIP If you are feeling anxious about your interview, remember that the company has chosen *you* from lots of other applicants.

Some recruitment processes are very quick and informal; others take longer and are more complex. Here are two case study examples of very different experiences.

Case Study 1
Saturday job in a café

Imran saw a job advertised at a café in the town centre. A short notice in the window gave only a few details about the role:

VACANCY for Saturday staff
Please contact manager for further details
Telephone: 012 345 6789

He went into the café and asked one of the staff about the vacancy. The manager was not available that morning, but Imran was given some written details about the job. These included the hours of work and rate of pay. There was also a brief description of the key tasks, which included:

- taking orders from customers
- clearing tables
- handling payments.

Imran telephoned in the afternoon and spoke to the manager. They needed someone who could start as soon as possible and he was invited for a short interview the following day.

Imran made sure that he looked tidy and smart for his interview and took a copy of his CV with him. The interview took place in the café itself at one of the tables. The manager was prepared to offer some training, but wanted someone who would be reliable.

So Imran highlighted that he had done a paper round for three years and could provide a reference. He also explained that the job would be ideal, as it would fit around his study commitments. The manager offered him a one-month trial and he started work the following week.

Case Study 2
Graduate engineering role

Hayley began looking for a job during the first term of the final year of her engineering course. She applied for a variety of graduate training posts with large national and international companies.

Her applications had to be submitted online and required a lot of detailed information, including:

- why she wanted to work as an engineer for that particular organisation
- details about a research project that she had completed
- confirmation of her commitment to further training.

She had to complete these applications whilst continuing to study for her degree course. Two of her applications were successful. She was then asked to complete some online selection tests for each of these.

One of the companies invited her to an assessment centre at a hotel. This major one-day event included:

- a face-to-face interview
- a group interview
- a variety of psychometric tests.

Hayley was delighted to receive a telephone call offering her the job. This was followed up with a letter of appointment and a detailed employment contract.

The recruitment process had taken a total of four months to complete.

The information that you provide on a CV or application form can certainly help a company pick out who might be best able to do the job. However, it can be harder to decide who to finally select and this is where interviews come in: by meeting you, companies can find out a lot more about you.

For example, an interviewer can:

- see how you present yourself
- observe how you communicate with other people

- find out why you want the job
- ask you more detailed questions about your skills and qualifications
- find out about a special project, course or job that you have done.

Meeting people and interviewing them can help interviewers make the right decision about who to choose. After all, they are going to spend a lot of money paying and perhaps training somebody to do that job. Companies therefore commit a great deal of time and expense to holding interviews. They do this in order to find the best person to do a job for them.

What happens at job interviews?

Job interviews are a very useful way for companies to find the right person to work for them. They may not, however, involve you actually doing the job itself. Instead, you might discuss different aspects of the job with an interviewer and be asked questions about things like your qualifications, skills and any work experience you have. You may also be asked to do some selection tests to check your knowledge or skills.

However, your interview:

- might not take place where the job is located – sometimes interviews are held in an office away from the main workplace, or even in a completely different town
- might not be with the person you will be working with – the interviewer may be from the company's HR department or a recruitment agency.

So interviews can feel a rather strange event that has little to do with the daily work a job might involve. Everybody can therefore feel a bit uncomfortable and they also feel that they have to be on their best behaviour – and that includes the interviewers!

TIP Interviews can be very different from doing the job and this is why they need some special preparation.

The company may be keen to tell you all about the best things that it can offer, and you will be trying to impress them too. And this can make it hard to relax, especially if it is your first job interview.

However, interviewers will understand that you might be nervous and will try to help you feel as welcome and comfortable as possible.

What are interviewers looking for?

One of the most helpful things to keep in mind is that interviewers *want* to find someone to do the job that is on offer.

For example:

- they may have lots of work piling up because someone has left the company
- they may have a new project that they need to get under way
- they may have a training programme ready for someone to start.

So they will be really hoping to find the right person on the interview day. By selecting you for an interview, they have therefore already decided that you are one of the best candidates for the job. They will be looking forward to meeting you and finding out more about you.

TIP Interviewers want to offer someone the job, so your aim is to help them see that you could do it.

Interviewers will therefore have some questions that they want to ask you, and they will be interested in your answers. They will not be planning to ask you lots of difficult or 'trick' questions – just ones that will help them to decide who may be able to do the job best.

This is why it is so important to do some careful planning – it will ensure that you make the best case possible for your suitability for the job.

Who will be interviewing you?

It can also be useful to think about things from the point of view of the person who is interviewing you. In particular, remember that interviewers are ordinary people just like you.

- They eat breakfast.
- They have a favourite TV show.
- They get worried and stressed about things too!

Remember that while some interviewers may have lots of experience at interviewing people, others may not. They may feel very confident about being an interviewer, or possibly be a bit nervous about it. They probably also have a long and busy day of interviews ahead of them.

So if you can present clear and relevant information about yourself, it will help the interviewer to understand your suitability for and interest in the job.

What do you want from the interview?

The simple answer to this question is, of course, to be offered the job! But just how do you go about convincing an interviewer that you are the best candidate?

One important way is to be very clear yourself about why you want the job and what you can offer.

TIP If you are going to convince an interviewer to offer you a job, you must first convince yourself that you can do it.

And this is *not* about being super-confident, or being the best-dressed candidate. It *is* about doing some careful preparation to identify key points that you want the interviewer to know about you. These could include:

- a relevant skill that will help you do the job
- a special project that you have studied
- the commitment you have shown to playing a sport
- what you have enjoyed and learned from being in a school show
- the skills you developed through helping to organise an event.

By doing some preparation, you are more likely to remember important examples of things like qualifications, skills or interests. You will also be able to talk about these in a way that helps convince the interviewer that you are the best candidate. You can then ensure that you come out of your interview knowing that you have highlighted all the best reasons why you could do the job.

TIP Try thinking about an interview as a two-way conversation and a chance for you to find out if you would be happy working for this company.

Interviews can also be a chance for you to find out more about things like:

- the job
- the company
- the people you will be working with.

So it can help a lot to think about interviews being a two-way conversation between you and the interviewer. They are an opportunity for you to ask some questions too, and ensure that this is a job that you will be happy doing.

How will the interviewer decide who to offer the job to?

It is likely that you will be one of a group of people being interviewed. So once the interviewer has met everyone, they will have to choose someone to offer the job to.

Ideally there will be a candidate who has exactly the set of skills and qualities that the job requires. Sometimes two different candidates may have a similar set of skills, however, and it can be difficult to decide who to appoint.

Interviewers will therefore use a variety of information to make their final decision. This will include things like:

- your skills and qualifications
- the results of any selection tests or practical exercises
- how you answer the interview questions that they ask
- how you speak and behave during the interview.

Interviewers can also be influenced by things like their first impressions of meeting you and the type of personality they think you display during the interview. They will try to be as objective as possible. However, selecting the right person can sometimes be hard and different interviewers may even prefer different people. So interviews are actually quite complicated events. Preparing thoroughly for them, however, can ensure that you:

- feel more confident
- give clear and concise information
- present this information as convincingly as possible

■ help the interviewer to understand why they should
   appoint you.

Next steps

This chapter has looked at what interviews are all about – from
the point of view of both the interviewer and the interviewee. It
has also asked you to start thinking about your own interview
and how you feel about it. And it has highlighted why it can be
so useful to do some preparation.

The next stage is to think about just what sort of preparation
you might need to do. This will depend on your own queries
and concerns, but also on how much time you have before
your interview.

The next chapter will help you to draw up your own personalised
interview plan.

Checklist: what are interviews all about?

                                                  ✔

Understand why companies have interviews   ☐

Consider the interviewer's point of view   ☐

Identify what you are looking forward to about your
interview   ☐

Identify any concerns you have about your interview   ☐

Understand the importance of interview preparation   ☐

---

2 PLANNING FOR SUCCESS

Doing the right kind of preparation before your first interview will really help to ensure that you do yourself justice on the big day.

So what kind of interview preparation should you be doing and how long will it take? There are lots of different types of preparation and everyone will have different requirements. You therefore need to spend time drawing up a focused plan to suit your needs.

This chapter will help you to develop a clear strategy for your interview preparation. It will enable you to identify which preparation is best for you. It will also take into account how much time you have available and how to schedule your preparation.

This chapter will:

- help you draw up a plan that fits your own needs and timescales
- identify different types of interview preparation
- identify different stages of interview preparation
- explain how to schedule your interview preparation
- offer time-saving tips for interview preparation.

Starting point

The best time to start planning your preparation is as soon as you are offered an interview. However, a company may have invited you at short notice. Or perhaps you are really busy with study deadlines, or other commitments.

So how can you make sure that you are ready for your first interview? And what if your interview is a month away, or tomorrow . . .?

There are several things that you need to consider:

- what types of preparation you should focus on
- your own key interview priorities
- how much time you have available
- who might be able to help you.

It is therefore vital to begin by spending some time planning your preparation strategy. This will not be wasted time, as it will ensure that you focus on the *right* preparation.

The following sections include exercises that are designed to help you develop a personalised and effective plan.

What interview preparation should I do?

There is a wide variety of preparation that you can do for an interview. You therefore need to understand what the key types are and decide which are the most relevant for you.

The following exercise asks you to check through a list of different aspects of preparation. This will help you to think about what you may need to do. It will also point you to the relevant chapters in this book where you can find more information to help you with your preparation.

EXERCISE 1

As you read through the following list, consider each point carefully and think about how important it might be for you.

	Very	Fairly	Not at all	Chapter
Interview and travel arrangements				
Check and confirm interview arrangements	☐	☐	☐	Chapter 3
Set up file for interview paperwork	☐	☐	☐	Chapter 3
Organise travel arrangements	☐	☐	☐	Chapter 3
Decide what to wear	☐	☐	☐	Chapter 3
The interview itself				
Review your application	☐	☐	☐	Chapter 3
Find out more about the job	☐	☐	☐	Chapter 3
Find out more about the company	☐	☐	☐	Chapter 3
Identify the type of interview format	☐	☐	☐	Chapter 4
Prepare for any selection tests	☐	☐	☐	Chapter 5
Prepare for interview questions	☐	☐	☐	Chapters 9, 10
Presentation skills				
Work on positive first impressions	☐	☐	☐	Chapter 6
Practise body language	☐	☐	☐	Chapter 6
Identify unique selling point	☐	☐	☐	Chapter 7
Practise relaxation techniques	☐	☐	☐	Chapter 8

What are my key interview issues?

It is also very important to think about your own key interview queries and concerns. This can help you decide what order to do your preparation in. And if you are short of time, it can help you to focus on your most important priorities.

Perhaps you are concerned about the questions you might be asked at your interview, but there is a particular question that really worries you. Or you may be anxious about the travel arrangements, having to do a test at the interview, or be uncertain what to wear.

You may have one main issue on your mind, or several different ones. You are also likely to need to focus on different aspects of interview preparation from anybody else – such as other candidates, or your friends.

Here are some examples.

- You already know a lot about the company, but need to do some work on confidence building.
- You want to spend more time thinking about 'Top 10' questions, rather than shopping for a new outfit if you already have something suitable to wear.

The following exercise will therefore ask you to think about your own personal interview queries and concerns.

EXERCISE 2

Take a few minutes to consider how you feel about your interview.

Also refer back to Chapter 1, where we asked you to think about which aspects of your interview you were looking forward to, or concerns that you might have.

Whether your interview issues seem big or small, have a think about the **five main things that concern you** and write them down in order of priority.

How much time do I have?

The first two exercises will have helped you think about the types of interview preparation you would find it useful to do and about your own personal priorities. They will also have given you some idea of how much preparation you may need to undertake.

If you have plenty of time before your interview, you may be able to fit all of this in. Your 'To Do' list may be much longer than you anticipated, however, or you may be very short of time.

So the following exercise will help you to be realistic about how much time you have available for interview preparation.

EXERCISE 3

How much time you have to prepare for your interview will depend on two key things. The first is whether your interview is very soon, or several weeks away. And the second is how busy you are likely to be in the run-up to your interview.

So have a look through your diary and then answer the following questions.

1. How long is it until my interview?
    Less than a week ☐
    One week ☐
    A few weeks ☐

2. How many hours/days can I give to interview preparation?
    _____ hours
    _____ days
    _____ evenings
    _____ weekends

Who might be able to help?

People are usually very happy to help when they know that your first interview is coming up, so it is well worth thinking about who might be able to assist you with your preparation – for example family, friends, a teacher, tutor, or careers adviser.

Perhaps someone could help you with some research, interview practice or travel plans? You might find it useful just to talk to someone if you are feeling a bit anxious about your interview. Or you may simply want a second opinion about what to wear.

EXERCISE 4

Begin by looking back through Exercise 1 and Exercise 2 and think about anyone who might be able to help.

You may want help with one particular aspect of your interview preparation, such as your travel plans.

There might also be someone – such as a careers adviser – who can help with a variety of different aspects of your preparation.

Now have a think about people you know who could help you with your preparation and write down their names and what they might be able to assist with.

Your own personal plan

Now you are ready to start developing a more focused plan to prepare for your first interview. This will draw on information from the exercises you have completed.

So work through the following key steps to help you create your own personalised plan.

■ **Step 1 'Must do' tasks**

Everyone is likely to benefit from doing some particular types of preparation. So even if you are short of time, do try and include the following in your plan:

- checking interview and travel arrangements
- reviewing your job application
- preparing for some interview questions.

■ **Step 2 Personal priorities**

You will also have your own personal priorities and concerns about your interview. So make sure you include in your plan anything that you identified in Exercise 1 and Exercise 2.

This could be just one small query, or a longer list of things to work on. The important thing here is to include anything that really matters to *you*.

■ **Step 3 Scheduling**

Some types of preparation take much more time than others. For example, checking your interview arrangements will not take long. Preparing and practising a talk, however, is going to take more time.

Aim to start work on the more important and time-consuming tasks first. Then see if there are some other things that you can leave until nearer the interview day.

■ **Step 4 Time savers**

Be realistic about what you can do in the time you have available. If you are at school, college or work during the day, for example, make use of time in the evenings or at weekends.

You may feel that you have plenty of time to prepare; or you may be concerned that you are very short of time.

So now review your answers to Exercise 3. If you do not have much time before your interview, think about some time savers:

- cancel or rearrange a social arrangement
- book some time off work, or take some flexi-time

- borrow a bag or coat, instead of going on a time-consuming shopping trip
- ask someone to help you with your preparation.

- **Step 5 Talking to people**

  If you need to contact people to help you with your interview preparation, explain carefully what help you need and what your timescale is.

  Remember that although a friend may be able to do something straight away, you may have to book an appointment with someone like a teacher or a careers adviser. So allow time to get in touch with people and arrange a meeting with them.

Drawing up your own personal plan

If you do have several weeks to prepare, you can draw up a timetable of things to do at different stages before your interview. So you might think about what you can do:

- when you first hear that you have an interview
- a week before your interview
- the day before your interview
- on the day itself.

Here are some countdown checklists to get you started. Use these as a basis for drawing up your own personalised plan.

Countdown checklists

When you first hear that you have an interview

Read through interview information carefully ☐
Check interview date, time and location ☐
Set up an interview file ☐
Plan travel arrangements ☐
Plan interview outfit ☐

Review your job application ☐
Research job ☐
Research company ☐
Prepare interview questions/answers ☐
Practise a variety of selection tests ☐
Prepare presentation ☐
Begin mental preparation exercises ☐
Begin relaxation exercises ☐
Contact/meet anyone who can help with your interview ☐

One week before

Practise handshake ☐
Practise body language ☐
Practise presentation ☐
Practise interview questions/answers out loud ☐
Review job application ☐
Review job research ☐
Review company research ☐
Continue practising selection tests ☐
Continue mental preparation exercises ☐
Continue relaxation exercises ☐
Ensure clothes are washed, collected from dry cleaners ☐
Write a checklist of what to take on the day ☐

The day before

Read job application ☐
Read job and company research ☐
Read through interview questions and answers ☐
Final practice of presentation ☐
Collect cash/change required ☐
Iron and put out clothes ☐
Clean shoes ☐
Pack bag/briefcase ☐
Relaxation exercises ☐
Have a reasonably early night! ☐
Set your alarm ☐
Charge your mobile phone ☐

On the day

Allow plenty of time ☐
Have breakfast ☐
Final bag check ☐
Follow travel plans ☐
Arrive at interview ☐
Switch off your phone ☐
Relaxation technique ☐
Mirror check ☐
Smile!!! ☐

Short of time?

If you are very short of time, choose the most important and practical things that you can do in the hours available.

For example, always check and think through the timings of your interview and travel plans – you need to turn up on time.

Also think about multi-tasking – perhaps you could check through your job application over breakfast, or practise interview questions on the way to the interview.

Any preparation will be helpful, so aim to make the best use of even one hour of time. Even this could improve significantly your chances of landing the job.

Case Study 1

Zoe: several weeks' notice of a formal interview, including a presentation

Although Zoe's interview for a retail management scheme was some time away, she had a lot of study deadlines to manage as well. She therefore decided to do most of her interview preparation at the weekends. She also drew up a detailed schedule of things that she needed to do to prepare for her interview. Zoe was particularly anxious about giving a presentation and therefore made this task a priority. So she wrote her presentation during the first weekend – and then practised it in front of members of her family during each of the remaining weekends.

Case Study 2

Hayley: last-minute invitation to an informal interview

Hayley returned home from college for the summer holidays hoping to find some temporary work. She heard from a neighbour that a local farmer was looking for staff to help with fruit picking, so she telephoned and was invited for a short interview the following day. She cancelled her plans to meet friends that evening; instead, she spent the time updating a short CV that she had prepared a couple of years ago for a school work experience scheme. She included two current references who would be happy to be contacted.

Case Study 3

Mark: balancing organising an interview outfit with other interview preparation

Mark had one week's notice of an interview for an office apprenticeship with a company that he really wanted to work for. He knew that he would be up against some other well-qualified applicants, so he wanted to look smart for his interview: but he also needed time to work on his interview questions and answers. Mark talked to his mum and she offered to take him shopping for a suit and tie after school one day. He also borrowed a briefcase from his older brother. This left the weekend clear to do the rest of his interview preparation.

Next steps

The type and amount of interview preparation that you need to do will depend on lots of different things. A formal day of interviews including selection tests and giving a presentation is likely to involve a lot more work, for example, than a short interview.

This chapter has covered the main types and stages of preparation that you need to think about. By working through the various exercises, you will have succeeded in drawing up a clear and focused timetable.

Now that you have your own personalised plan, the following chapter will help you to start work on the interview preparation itself.

Checklist: planning for success

	✔
Identify which types of interview preparation you need to do	☐
Identify your interview preparation priorities	☐
Decide how much time you can spend on interview preparation	☐
Draw up your own personalised plan	☐
Include a countdown checklist	☐
Think about interview preparation time savers	☐

---

3 PREPARATION, PREPARATION, PREPARATION!

The previous chapter highlighted many different things that you can do to prepare for an interview. These range from practical tasks and research to mental preparation. This chapter will look in more detail at how to prepare for your interview.

Some things may seem pretty obvious, such as checking exactly when and where your interview is being held. But sadly, people do turn up late or on the wrong day and miss their interview opportunity.

The aim of your preparation is to make sure that you build on the good impression that your job application has already made. You also want to avoid making any big mistakes at the interview that could really let you down on the day.

Once you have planned out what interview preparation you need to do, just how do you get started? This chapter will take you through a step-by-step guide to some initial areas of preparation and provide checklists for each of them. It will:

■ identify key areas of interview preparation
■ highlight important initial tasks and how to undertake them
■ explain what steps to take to get your interview preparation under way
■ provide checklists for each area of initial interview preparation.

Key areas of interview preparation

There are a lot of different types of interview preparation. Some of them are vital for every interview, such as checking the date, time and location of your appointment. You also need to make careful travel plans.

Many other aspects of interview preparation are also important, although the time you spend on them will depend on your own needs and timescales.

Some initial areas of interview preparation include:

- interview arrangements
- paperwork
- travel plans
- reviewing your job application
- finding out about the job
- researching the company
- sorting out what to wear.

The following sections in this chapter will describe each of these aspects in more detail. This will help you get your interview preparation under way. Further information about other preparation topics is included in subsequent chapters.

So focus on those areas of preparation that you identified in your personal plan – developed through undertaking the exercises in Chapter 2.

Interview arrangements

If you have a letter or email inviting you to an interview, read it through carefully. If you are invited by telephone, write down any details as soon as possible.

Then make sure that you put the correct information on the calendar or your electronic diary. In the excitement of hearing that you have an interview, it can be easy to misread something!

Make sure that you check the following very carefully:

■ date of your interview
■ time of your interview
■ location of your interview.

Also consider at this stage if you are unsure about any of these arrangements. Your interview letter should give you all the necessary details and you may even have been sent a map.

However, you could feel unclear about things such as:

■ how long your interview will take
■ where your interview is taking place
■ what type of interview you will have
■ what type of selection tests you may have to do
■ how many people will be interviewing you.

So write down here any queries that you have about the interview arrangements at this stage:

You may need to contact the company if there is something really important that you need to check. A good time to do this is when you reply to the company to confirm that you will be attending the interview. You might have to reply by telephone or email – and there may be a deadline for your reply – so you could use this opportunity to ask about any of the interview arrangements.

Most companies will be happy to help with any sensible queries. For example, you might need to know roughly how long your interview will take so that you can make travel arrangements for getting back to school, college or work.

Interview arrangements checklist

	✔
Read through any interview information carefully	☐
Check date, time and location of interview	☐
Enter the time/date in your diary	☐
Write down any queries about your interview arrangements	☐
Confirm that you are attending the interview	☐
Check any interview arrangements with the company	☐

Paperwork

You will probably collect a surprising number of important letters and information in the run-up to your interview.

Some key paperwork will include:

- interview information provided by the company
- your job application
- your own interview research and notes
- travel information and tickets.

The last thing you want to do is to lose a vital piece of paper. So set up a file or online folder to keep all your interview notes and paperwork safe. Being organised like this can also help you to feel in better control of your interview preparation.

Paperwork checklist

✔

Job advert ☐

Job description ☐

Person specification ☐

Job application ☐

Interview letter/emails ☐

Your interview preparation schedule ☐

Notes about the job, company, questions ☐

Travel timetables and tickets ☐

Travel plans

It is vital to think very carefully about your travel plans. You must ensure that you arrive in good time for your interview and on the right day. Although this sounds obvious, one of the most common problems reported by interviewers is that candidates arrive late.

Even if you know exactly where the company is, it is useful to double-check travel times. You could consider visiting the location beforehand if it is not too far away. And work back from your interview appointment time to check what time you actually need to leave home.

You should *always* make sure that you have a back-up plan in case there are any problems with your transport. For example, if a bus or train is delayed, perhaps you could ask a friend or relation to be on stand-by to give you a lift.

Checklist: working out your travel plans

Time of my interview: _____

Step 1 Aim to arrive approximately 15 minutes early for your interview.

Arrival time at company: _____

Step 2 Work out how long it will take to travel from your home to the interview (include time for, e.g., parking your car, walking to/from bus stop, getting to/from train station):

Travel time: _____

Step 3 Decide whether you need to allow extra time for any delays – this can be particularly important if you have a long journey to make. You might decide, for example, to catch an earlier train, or start your car journey a little bit earlier:

Extra time allowance: _____

Step 4 Work out your departure time, taking into account your travel time and any extra time allowance you decide to include:

Departure time: _____

If you are travelling some distance, you may need to book coach or train tickets in advance. Always keep your receipts because some companies will refund your travel costs, but they will need evidence of how much you paid.

If you are not sure about the exact location of the company, look it up on a street map or the internet. Do this even if you plan to drive – sat navs are *not* foolproof!

TIP Remember to have the contact details of the company with you in case you need to contact them about an unexpected delay.

If you are driving, check out parking arrangements, particularly if the company does not have its own car park. Find out where the nearest public car parks are located. You may also need the correct change or a debit/credit card to pay for parking.

Even the best travel plans can go wrong – a major train delay, traffic hold-up, or a car breakdown. If this happens, try to keep calm. Contact the company as soon as you can to let them know what is happening. It may be possible to rearrange your interview for later in the day, or perhaps even hold it on another day.

Travel plans checklist

	✔
Check where the interview is being held	☐
Decide which form of transport to use	☐
Work out travel times	☐
Look up bus/coach/train timetables	☐
Book travel tickets in advance	☐
Check parking arrangements, charges and payment method	☐
Organise a travel back-up plan	☐

Reviewing your job application

It may seem rather unnecessary to suggest that you read through your job application – after all, you spent a lot of time writing it!

However, the interviewer is very likely to ask you some questions based on your application. And if your interview is some time away, it can be easy to forget a lot of the details. So read through all the information that you have, including the original job advertisement and any job description and person specification you were sent.

Also go carefully through your CV and/or application form. While you do this, try to put yourself in the interviewer's place. In particular, think about what your job application might prompt them to ask you to talk about.

For example, start to think about any questions they might ask about your:

- skills
- qualifications
- work experience
- interests.

Also look out for anything on your CV that may need some further explanation. This could be something that needs clarification such as where you studied for a qualification, or why there is a gap in your study or work history.

And an interviewer might want to hear more about an interesting project that you undertook, or a gap year or voluntary project that you worked on.

Review of job application checklist

	✔
Read through job information	☐
Read through your job application	☐
Highlight points the interviewer might ask about	☐
Check any further information you may need to provide	☐

Finding out about the job

You may feel reasonably clear about what a job will involve. And an interview can be a good opportunity for you to find out more about a job. So why should you think about doing any further research before your interview?

Certainly if you have a detailed job advert, job description or person specification you will have a good idea about the role. Or perhaps you have done some relevant work experience and have carried out many of the key tasks involved.

However, not all companies provide much information about a job. And even if they do, this still may not tell you everything that you need to know.

For example:

- job titles can be unclear
- jobs can vary in terms of tasks, responsibilities and pay levels
- jobs may be temporary or permanent
- training opportunities can vary.

So a job advertised as an 'Office Assistant' may be a temporary job doing some filing. Or it could be an Apprenticeship training post covering a range of administrative work.

Knowing this sort of information about a job can help you to prepare for your interview. This includes thinking about questions you might be asked at your interview about the job itself – as well as questions that you would like to ask the interviewer.

Some useful things to find out include:

- key tasks and responsibilities
- key skills and qualifications

- training opportunities
- career progression
- professional qualifications
- salary levels.

There are lots of different ways to find out more about a job. You can research relevant jobs and careers more generally and also within the company that is offering the interview.

Try checking out:

- careers websites
- careers library at school or college
- public library
- recruitment websites
- company website
- company brochures.

Training and professional organisations often provide very useful information about jobs, careers and training schemes. It can also be really helpful to talk to someone who does a similar job. Most people are happy to discuss what they do, so ask friends and family if they know anyone.

Look out for further information via:

- Sector Skills Councils
- training organisations
- professional organisations
- someone who does this sort of work.

Job research checklist

	✔
Decide what job information will be useful	☐
Highlight points the interviewer might ask about	☐

Do some research about the job using:

■ careers websites/publications	☐
■ company website/publications	☐
■ training websites/publications	☐
■ careers and public libraries	☐
■ personal contacts	☐

Researching the company

You may have applied for similar jobs with a variety of different companies, but at an interview the company will want to know why you want to work for *them*.

This can make a big difference at your interview because:

- ■ *if you do not know much about the company* you can seem disinterested and poorly informed and this can really put an interviewer off
- ■ *if you have taken the time to find out about the company* you will appear well informed and committed to doing the job.

Doing some research about the company is therefore really important, but what do you need to find out? This depends on the type of job that you have applied for and the size of the company, but some useful things include:

- ■ what the company does – key products and services
- ■ how big the company is – number of employees, turnover
- ■ where it is based – different locations, UK only or overseas
- ■ key departments
- ■ key staff
- ■ new company projects
- ■ recent news items
- ■ general industry trends/issues.

There are lots of different ways to find out about a company, especially if it is a larger organisation, but even smaller companies might have a website or produce some publications. Try checking out:

- company website
- company's annual report
- company brochures
- company's press releases
- leaflets about products and services.

You may be able to find out lots of information really quickly from a company website. Remember that there are plenty of other sources of information too, such as libraries, newspapers and magazines.

Also think about the wider industry or sector that the company may be a part of. Some companies have a trade association that represents their views, does research and develops policy. So look out for information via:

- the internet
- public library
- careers library at school or college
- newspapers
- trade magazines
- trade associations
- someone who knows about or works for the company.

Company research checklist

	✔
Decide what company information will be useful	☐

Do some research using:

	✔
the internet	☐
company publications	☐
trade publications	☐

- library ☐
- newspapers/magazines ☐
- personal contacts ☐

What am I going to wear?

Another important part of interview preparation is deciding what to wear. You also need to give some thought to your overall appearance. The general aim is to appear smart and professional.

Wearing the right outfit is really important because it can:

- help present the right visual impression to an interviewer
- help you to feel more confident.

This can mean looking a bit smarter than usual. However, you also need to ensure that you feel comfortable to enable you to focus on the interview itself. You do not want to find yourself distracted by an uncomfortable pair of new shoes, for example, or an item of clothing that is too tight.

TIP If you are unsure about what to wear, ask for advice from someone you know – and whose dress sense you trust!

For most interviews a smart skirt/trousers, jacket and blouse/shirt is appropriate. However, a suit and tie may be required for more formal interviews. In general, avoid high fashion items, low-cut tops and very short hemlines.

In order to decide what to wear, it can help to know the dress code for both the company you are hoping to work for and the job itself. And then aim for a 'smart' version of that.

You will also need a suitable bag and/or briefcase, shoes and possibly a coat. Do ensure that everything is clean and ironed, so schedule time for this and arrange for anything that needs to be dry cleaned to go to the dry cleaners in advance.

Ensuring that your general appearance is smart is just as important as your outfit. In particular, make sure that your hair and nails are cut, clean and tidy. And also check that any accessories are smart and polished – do not be let down by a scruffy bag, shoes or coat.

Do wear:
- clean and ironed clothes
- clean nails
- clean shoes
- tidy hair
- smart accessories

Don't wear:
- low-cut top or short skirt
- high fashion items
- too much make-up
- badly fitting clothes
- too much perfume/ aftershave

You may need to think about buying a new outfit, but it is possible that you have some of the right clothes and just need a few extra items. Also consider borrowing something like a smart coat or bag if you do not have much money to spend.

Finally, have a think about what you will need to carry with you on the day. This will help you to decide which bag/briefcase to take everything in.

What to take to your interview:

- mobile phone
- tickets, travel card
- money, change, credit cards
- paperwork (interview letter, job application)
- documentation (if requested, e.g. certificates, artwork)

- presentation materials (if required, e.g. USB stick, handouts)
- comb/hairbrush
- small mirror
- umbrella
- tissues
- bottle of water and snack if travelling
- spare shoelaces, tights
- keys.

Other: _____

_____

_____

Organising what to wear checklist

	✔
Think about the type of outfit and accessories	☐
Organise a time/day for a shopping trip	☐
Book hair appointment	☐
Take any items to the dry cleaners	☐
Wash/iron clothes	☐
Repair and clean shoes	☐
Write a list of things to take to your interview	☐

Next steps

Interview preparation can include a whole variety of tasks, from simple things, like checking the time and date of your interview, to going carefully through your job application beforehand.

This chapter has covered some initial types of preparation and how to go about them. Preparation is all about thinking and planning ahead, so use the checklists to ensure that you cover all the important points.

Now that you have got some preparation under way, the following chapters will help you to think about further aspects of interview preparation and how to handle the big day itself.

Checklist: preparation, preparation, preparation!

	✔
Check interview arrangements	☐
Set up file for paperwork	☐
Organise travel plans	☐
Review your job application	☐
Research the job	☐
Research the company	☐
Organise your interview outfit	☐

---

4 WHAT TYPE OF INTERVIEW?

Not all interviews follow one standard format. No two interviews will ever be exactly the same, and each interviewer will have their own personal approach.

Some interviews are very short and informal; at others you may find yourself facing several interviewers, or even having an interview with a group of other candidates.

Understanding the key features of these different types of interview is really important. This will help you to know what to expect. It will also inform your interview preparation and enable you to handle different interview situations.

Knowing about the various approaches to interviewing will therefore ensure that you are ready to deal with whatever arises.

This chapter will:

- explain why there are different types of interview
- identify a variety of interview formats
- discuss key features and how to handle them.

Why are there different types of interview?

As your career gets under way you are likely to find yourself invited to different types of interview. And when you talk to other people, you will hear about a wide variety of interview experiences. So why do interview formats and experiences vary so much? It is because the type of interview can depend a lot on:

- the kind of job that you have applied for
- the type of company

- the size of company
- the person interviewing you.

You might find yourself having a telephone interview, meeting an interviewer face to face, or even being interviewed by a panel. Interviewers are all individuals, so their personal style can also have an impact on your interview experience.

Different interview formats

Example 1

A company asks a recruitment agency to screen applicants via short telephone interviews, then follow up with face-to-face interviews.

Example 2

A small company seeking a junior member of staff arranges for a face-to-face interview with one of their managers.

Example 3

For a job that involves working with several departments, a large company holds panel interviews to enable more staff to meet the applicants.

You may not know the exact format of your interview beforehand. Some companies will provide detailed information about this, but others do not. You may also find yourself being invited to a second, or follow-up, interview, as part of some recruitment processes.

Some interviewers and companies are also very experienced at holding interviews, while others have done very little interviewing. Some interviews may therefore follow a very clear format, but others may not be so well organised.

So it can help to be prepared for the unexpected when you are invited to an interview! One way of doing this is to understand the different types of interview that you might come across. These include:

- one-to-one interviews
- informal interviews
- telephone interviews
- panel interviews
- group interviews.

One-to-one interviews

These are one of the most common types of interview. They involve meeting an interviewer face to face and discussing your job application and suitability for the job.

This type of interview often follows a fairly standard format. It will include a number of key stages, starting from the moment you arrive at a company and closing with the end of your interview.

Interviews: key stages

1. Arrival

- Arrive at company/interview reception area.
- Sign in (you may be asked to wear an identity badge).
- Wait in reception area, office, or outside the interview room.

2. Introductions

- Accompanied to interview room by interviewer/member of staff.
- Walk in and shake hands/greet interviewer.
- Introductions.

3. Main interview

- Interviewer outlines interview format.
- Some introductory questions.
- Main questions.
- You ask questions.

4. Departure

- Goodbyes.
- Return to reception area and sign out.

Thinking about your interview in this way can be really useful as there are some important points to look out for at each of these stages.

1. Arrival

Always try to arrive in good time. This is partly good manners, but it can also give you some valuable time in which to relax and prepare for your interview.

Also be aware that your interview begins from the moment you arrive at the company or interview location. Receptionists and any other staff that you meet may be asked their opinion of you. It is therefore important to be polite and friendly with everybody you meet.

So once you have arrived, what sort of things can you be doing and thinking about whilst waiting for your interview?

You can use this time to do some practical things such as switching off your mobile. Also try to relax a bit and consider your first impressions of the company and staff while you are waiting for your interview. Ask yourself, 'Is this somewhere I would like to work?'

Arrival checklist

	✔
Turn off your phone	☐
Go to the bathroom/mirror check	☐
Have a glass of water/drink	☐
Take a few deep breaths to relax	☐
Have a look through any company brochures	☐
Glance around the reception/waiting area	☐

2. Introductions

The interviewer may come out to meet you in reception, or a member of staff may take you along to the interview room.

Interview introductions may be rather more formal than you are used to. For example, in your everyday life you may not often have to shake hands with someone. An interview, however, is certainly an occasion when you are likely to have to do this.

So be prepared to:

- introduce yourself using your full name – first name and surname
- shake hands with the interviewer
- wait for the interviewer to invite you to sit down.

Then make sure that you are sitting as comfortably as possible. It is usually a good idea to keep a jacket on, as it will look more professional. And do not keep a bag or briefcase on your lap – put it down by the side of your chair.

TIP See Chapter 6 for more details about how to make a really great first impression and the role of body language during your interview.

Now you are ready for the main part of your interview to start!

3. Main interview

The main part of your interview will be a question and answer session. And one of your key aims here is to answer all the questions as clearly and effectively as you can.

However, the interviewer will also be making some broader assessment about the sort of person they think you are.

So as well as answering any questions, you want to try to build up a good rapport with the interviewer. This can be very hard to imagine doing, especially before you meet them.

However, interviewers will be hoping to meet someone who is:

- business-like and professional
- knowledgeable about the job and company
- quietly confident
- approachable and friendly
- enthusiastic.

An interviewer may start by giving you some introductory information about the company, the job and the interview format. They may then ask you some icebreaker questions, before moving on to some more in-depth questions. There will usually be an opportunity for you to ask some questions towards the end of the interview.

TIP See Chapter 9 and Chapter 10 for more information about different types of interview questions and how to answer them.

During this main part of the interview you also want to maintain a good rapport with the interviewer. Make some eye contact with the interviewer when you speak. Also listen carefully to the questions that they ask and try to answer them as directly as possible.

> **Do:**
> - make good eye contact
> - sit comfortably
> - listen carefully to the questions
> - answer the questions clearly and concisely.
>
> **Don't:**
> - mumble or speak too quietly
> - fidget and shift around in your chair
> - crack jokes, be flippant or too 'clever'
> - speak badly about anyone.

Also be prepared for the fact that interviewers can vary enormously, both as individuals and in terms of how they run an interview.

For example, your interviewer might be:

- business-like and formal – gets straight on with the interview questions
- relaxed and friendly – chats for a few minutes before starting the interview
- very organised – explains the interview format carefully
- a bit flustered and anxious – may seem unsure what questions to ask.

The tone of the interview can therefore depend a lot on the sort of person interviewing you; and on whether they have done much interviewing before. So be aware of this and think about how you might respond to the following types of interviewer.

Match the interviewing style with the appropriate response.

1. If an interviewer is very business-like . . .
2. If an interviewer is relaxed and friendly . . .
3. If an interviewer seems flustered and anxious . . .
   A. Answer their questions calmly and check if you are unsure what they are asking about.
   B. Offer friendly responses, but stay focused for formal questions.
   C. Follow their lead and keep your answers professional and concise.

(Answers: 1C, 2B, 3A.)

If an interviewer is more 'formal' or 'distant', you may feel that you are not doing very well. However, this could simply be the interviewer's style – so try to avoid reading too much into their manner and tone of voice.

Finally, do be prepared for your interviewer to take notes while you are talking. This can feel rather distracting, but it is often very useful for the interviewer to have a written record of the discussion.

4. Goodbyes

Again, this is likely to be a more formal process than you are used to. Remember to thank the interviewer for their time and shake hands.

Remember to take any belongings with you, such as a bag or coat. Also thank and say goodbye to any other staff on your way out of the building, including anyone who accompanies you out of your interview, or reception staff.

A formal interview:
- has a clear structure
- includes a standard set of questions
- takes place in the workplace/office.

An informal interview:
- does not have a clear format
- can seem more like a chat
- may take place away from the workplace/office.

Informal interviews

One-to-one interviews can vary a great deal in terms of how they are organised. In particular, some interviews may be very formal, whilst others may seem much more like a chat.

Both types of interview, however, require exactly the same kind of careful preparation. Just because an interview is informal does not mean that you can turn up without doing any planning or research.

And informal interviews actually require some special care, because it can be easy to forget that you are being interviewed!

So avoid being drawn into giving away more information than you wish, perhaps about your home or social life. In an interview, companies should only ask you questions that are relevant to the job. However, in an informal situation it can be easy to be drawn into more general conversations.

Therefore make sure that you stay alert and answer questions just as thoughtfully as you would in a more formal interview setting.

Panel interviews

At some interviews you may find yourself faced with more than one interviewer. These are called panel interviews and there could be two, three or more interviewers.

Panel interviews can feel a bit more stressful than one-to-one interviews, simply because you are outnumbered. However, understanding how they work can help you to feel more in control. In particular, it can be useful to know who is on the interview panel and their role in the interview.

The panel may be made up of a variety of people from the company, such as:

■ team leader
■ head of department
■ HR representative.

The interviewers on the panel may also have different roles.

Usually one person will be in charge of the interview panel and take the lead in organising everything. So they may carry out the introductions and explain the format of the interview to you.

Different people on the panel may then take it in turns to ask you different questions. What they ask you may depend on their job – or they may simply have divided a set of questions between them.

Here are some examples of how an interview panel might divide questions.

- *team leader* – wants to know more about your skills and ability to do the day-to-day job
- *head of department* – wants to know about your future career plans
- *HR representative* – asks about your qualifications and training issues.

There are also some benefits to a panel interview, although this may not seem the case when you are faced with more than one interviewer! For example:

■ you get to meet a wider variety of people from the company
■ you can find out information directly from the people involved
■ more than one person is assessing you, which can be fairer.

Panel interviews will follow a similar format to one-to-one interviews: introductions, questions and answers, then good-byes.

As with one-to-one interviewers, some panel interviews may be better run and organised than others. In a well-managed panel interview, the interviewers will ask questions in a set order. Be prepared, however, for different panel members to ask follow-up questions.

One of the most difficult aspects of a panel interview can be who to look at when you are answering a question. As a general rule:

■ address your reply to the person who has asked the question
■ glance at other members of the panel occasionally if you are answering a series of questions from one person.

Towards the end of the interview, direct your own final questions (if you have any) to whoever has led the interview panel. Another member of the panel can then always help to answer the question if this is appropriate.

Telephone interviews

Telephone interviews are often used to screen a larger group of job applicants. This can help a company to decide who they will then invite to a face-to-face interview.

Telephone interviews are often used to ask some preliminary questions. The interviewer might be interested in checking that you meet the right criteria, for example:

- correct qualifications
- suitable skills
- relevant work experience.

The interviewer may be someone from the company, or sometimes a recruitment agency working on their behalf.

They will usually arrange a date and time to telephone you, which, unlike face-to-face interviews, means that you do not have to spend time thinking about travel arrangements.

However, you do need to give some careful thought to how and where to take the call. You will need to provide the interviewer with a telephone number where they can easily contact you. This may be your mobile number, or a landline such as a home telephone number.

Do ensure that:

- you provide the correct telephone number
- the telephone is fully charged
- you answer the telephone yourself
- you speak clearly.

You also need to think about where to take the call. This is very important, as you do not want to have a telephone interview in a noisy place, or with other people around. So you will need:

- a quiet location, where you can concentrate and will not be disturbed
- a chair and desk/table, so that you can have your job application to hand and take notes.

Remember that telephone interviews are an important stage of the recruitment process. You want to make a good impression on the telephone and convince the interviewer that you can do the job.

This includes thinking about how to deal with introductions, a variety of interview questions and goodbyes. However, during a telephone interview both you and the interviewer have no visual information to help you.

During a telephone interview:

- you have less information about the person you are talking to
- you have no visual clues such as facial expressions or body language to help you see how the interviewer is responding to you
- your tone of voice and words become very important.

To check up on your telephone manner, ask someone you know how you sound on the telephone. In particular, make sure that you speak directly into the telephone and that your voice can be heard easily.

When the interviewer does call, make sure that *you* pick up the telephone. Answer clearly and professionally, giving your full name: 'Hello, _____ _____ speaking.'

Try to avoid long silences after you are asked a question. Instead, let the interviewer know what is happening by explaining that you are thinking about your answer.

You may also be given the opportunity to ask questions, so make sure that you have prepared for this. And as with any other interview, end the telephone interview politely by thanking the interviewer for their time.

Remember: you therefore need to do just as much preparation for a telephone interview as for any other type of interview.

If nobody telephones you at the correct time, do wait for someone to call – the interviewer may be running a little late. Allow about half an hour, then telephone the company yourself if you have not heard anything. Leave your name, a contact number and a message for the interviewer if you cannot speak to them direct.

On the day of your telephone interview:
- get up and dressed in good time
- take a few moments quietly beforehand to focus your thoughts
- switch off any other telephones
- sit comfortably at a table
- have your job application, pen and paper to hand
- have a glass of water nearby
- answer the telephone yourself.

Group interviews

A group interview involves being interviewed with other candidates who have applied for the job.

You might be given:

- ■ a topic to discuss
- ■ a task to do
- ■ a role-play exercise.

There will usually be a time limit, and one or more interviewers will observe you. Group interviews often require you to work together with other candidates under time pressure – and come up quickly with both ideas and solutions.

This format gives the interviewer a valuable opportunity to see how you interact with others and work as part of a team.

Group interviews can feel more stressful than other interview formats because:

- you may not know what you will be asked to do
- you will probably not know the other interviewees
- you may not be sure exactly what the interviewers are looking for.

It is important to remember that the most successful candidate will *not* necessarily be the loudest, the most confident, or the one who says the most.

TIP If the interviewer is looking for some evidence of leadership skills, they will want someone who earns the respect of the team – not the most vocal.

What specific things might an interviewer be looking for? It could be different skills, personality traits, or teamwork roles. For example, group interviews will help an interviewer identify who can:

- come up with good ideas
- listen to everybody's point of view
- make informed decisions
- focus on a practical solution
- stay calm
- overcome problems
- turn things around with a new idea
- sum up a discussion effectively.

What the interviewer is looking for will depend on the type of job, team, or company that is being interviewed for. So check back to any information that you have about the job, as this will help you to identify what is required.

At a group interview:
- listen carefully to the task
- wait for a good opportunity to speak
- voice your ideas
- be respectful of the rest of the group
- speak clearly and make your points concisely
- keep track of where the task/discussion is going
- make positive and constructive contributions.

Think carefully about any task that you are given and aim to make a positive contribution. Also remember that everyone is likely to be feeling a bit anxious about a group interview.

Although group interviews can seem rather unpredictable and stressful, people often find that they actually enjoy them. It can certainly be really interesting to meet the other candidates; and this interview format also offers a chance to do something practical and to demonstrate your skills. So try to relax and contribute positively to whatever discussion or task you are asked to undertake.

Next steps

This chapter has looked at a variety of different interview formats and their key features. These range from a short, informal interview to a much more formal approach.

Understanding how these different formats work can really help you decide the best way to prepare for them. It will also enable you to feel more confident and able to deal with any unexpected situations.

You may just have one short interview ahead of you, or a variety of different interviews and even some selection tests.

So the following chapter will outline what kind of additional tests and tasks you may be asked to carry out.

Checklist: what type of interview?

	✔
Be aware of different interview formats	☐
Understand different interview stages	☐
Be prepared for different types of interviewer	☐
Check which type of interview you are attending	☐
Understand the key features of your interview format	☐

---

5 SELECTION TESTS AND ASSESSMENT CENTRES

As part of their recruitment process, a company may ask you to do some selection tests, or to give a presentation. They may also invite you along to an assessment centre for a whole day of interviews and tests.

Different types of selection test can help a company to find out more about you by testing particular skills and aptitudes. They can also be a useful way of testing everyone at the same time and under similar conditions.

However, they can feel rather like doing an exam and you may be unsure what to expect. So understanding what different selection tests involve can be useful. It is also a good idea to practise these tests beforehand.

Similarly it is important to spend time preparing and practising a presentation. Doing this can help you feel more confident. It can also improve your chances of doing well in a selection testing process.

This chapter will:

- help you to understand the purpose of selection tests
- describe different types of selection test
- identify ways to prepare for selection tests
- help you prepare and deliver an effective presentation
- explain assessment centre recruitment processes.

Selection tests

Selection tests may be used to help screen applicants prior to the interview stage. You may be asked, for example, to complete a series of online tests before being selected for an interview.

This type of testing may also take place on the same day that you are invited to an interview. You could be asked to attend for a morning, or even a day, of interviews and tests. This may take place at the company itself, or at a special assessment centre.

Selection tests can include:

- psychometric tests
- case study
- in-tray exercise.

You will only be asked to do selection tests for certain types of work. They cost a company time and money to carry out, so they are usually only used for jobs that require very specific skills, or for management posts.

A company will usually tell you in advance if you will have to do any selection tests or give a presentation. However, you may not be given many details beforehand and it is worth being prepared for a variety of different test processes.

Psychometric tests

These may sound rather technical (and scary), but they are basically written tests that aim to uncover more about your abilities and personality.

Psychometric tests will usually be held under exam conditions: there will be a time limit and no talking or discussion will be allowed.

Aptitude and ability tests

These are concerned with thinking and reasoning skills. There are different types that test:

- verbal skills
- numeracy skills
- abstract reasoning skills
- spatial skills
- mechanical skills

You may be asked to do one type of test or several different ones, depending on the sort of job you have applied for.

Often these tests check not only your knowledge, but also your ability to work under pressure. So also be prepared for the possibility that:

- the questions get harder as you go through a test
- you find it difficult to complete every question in the time allowed.

TIP There are lots of books and websites offering practice tests – do try some beforehand so that you know what to expect.

Good basic exam technique is also very important in order to do well in these tests, so remember to:

- read each question carefully
- write your answers carefully
- move on, if you cannot answer a question
- check your answers at the end if you have time.

Personality tests

Personality tests ask questions about how you might go about doing a task, or how you feel about something. There may be a time limit, but there are no right or wrong answers to personality tests. For example, your answers may suggest that you have a certain personality type – such as more outgoing, or more reflective. And a company will be looking for a personality type that will fit a job best.

These tests are carefully designed to make it difficult to work out any 'right' answer. So complete them as truthfully as possible and remember they are just one part of a wider recruitment process.

Case study

This is an exercise to find out how you would deal with a situation that might happen at work, or in everyday life. Often the topic will be a problem that might arise.

A simple case study might ask you to focus on one particular issue, such as:

- how to manage an angry customer in a shop
- what to do if a project for a client is behind schedule
- how to handle a member of staff who is always late for work.

More complex case studies can be about broader business or management problems. For example, they could concern how to advise a company that is no longer making a profit.

TIP A case study will usually be related to the type of job you have applied for.

You will be given some information about a case study to read through. This may be anything from a few lines to a set of detailed papers. After reading through the case study, you will be asked to discuss your ideas with the interviewer, or to provide a written answer.

The interviewer will be looking for evidence that:

■ you understand the problem
■ you can identify potential solutions
■ you can describe what you would do
■ you can explain your decisions.

Always begin by *carefully* reading through the case study. Then set out your ideas as clearly as possible. Make sure that you suggest practical solutions and can justify your proposals.

In-tray exercise

This type of exercise aims to see how well you can deal with lots of information and decide which are the most important tasks to prioritise.

You will usually be given an outline of your fictitious role in an organisation. This will often be a similar role to the job that you are being interviewed for. You will then be given a set of papers or emails that you have to read through and decide how to deal with.

An in-tray exercise might include:

• emails
• letters
• telephone messages
• company reports
• survey results.

There may be a time limit for this exercise and you could be under some pressure to complete a lot of work in a short time.

This can help the interviewer to see how you prioritise tasks, make decisions and draft replies to correspondence.

So aim to:

- scan through everything quickly first
- decide priorities and timescales
- identify where you can delegate
- structure any written replies
- pay attention to grammar and spelling.

You may be asked to discuss this exercise at your interview and explain why you took particular decisions.

However, there may not necessarily be a right or wrong way of doing this type of task. It can be more about seeing whether you can work in an orderly fashion and justify your approach.

Presentations

You may be asked to give a talk at your interview. It could just be for a few minutes, or a longer and more formal presentation. You may be given a subject to talk about or asked to choose a topic of your own.

Why might an interviewer want to hear you give a talk or presentation? It could be for a variety of reasons, for example:

- it is an important part of the job (e.g. teaching, giving sales presentations)
- to find out how much you know about a particular topic
- to assess your presentation skills more generally.

A presentation may be part of a wider recruitment process, so you will probably have an interview as well, which will usually take place on the same day.

If you are given any instructions about your presentation, read these through very carefully. In particular make sure you are clear about:

- topic
- time limits
- technology.

Your audience may be your interviewer(s), but it could also include other staff, or possibly other interview candidates. So if you prepare any handouts, take enough to ensure that everyone can have a copy. Check with the company about this beforehand if necessary.

Also check in advance whether you will be able to show slides, for example using PowerPoint. This can make your talk seem much more effective and professional. However, do not prepare too many slides, keep them simple and avoid too many distracting special effects.

TIP Be prepared to answer some questions from the audience at the end of your presentation.

You may feel a bit anxious about having to stand up and give a talk. However, it can help a lot to think carefully about your presentation beforehand and allow plenty of time for preparing it. Also practise giving your talk out loud to check timings and to see how it sounds.

When you are planning your presentation, make sure that you:

- choose a topic that is relevant to the job
- pick a topic that you are comfortable with
- allow time for research, preparation and practice
- structure your talk (introduction, key points, conclusions).

On the day, ensure that you take any information and items that you will need for your talk. These might include cue cards, a memory stick or a laptop.

Tips for an effective presentation

- Speak slowly and clearly.
- Look at your audience.
- Explain the structure of your talk.
- Stick to the topic.
- Keep overheads/slides simple and relevant.
- Use cue cards (do not read from a script).
- Avoid jargon or abbreviations.
- Keep to time limits.
- Ask at the end if there are any questions.

If you are asked any questions, keep your answers as focused as possible – just as you would for an interview question. Address your answer to the person who asked the question, but glance around at the rest of the audience briefly too.

Then thank everyone for listening, sit down and relax!

Assessment centres

If you are invited to an assessment centre, you might find yourself doing a variety of interviews, group exercises and selection tests over one or two days. This type of interview format is generally used by larger companies to screen and recruit candidates.

An assessment centre itself may be:

- ■ a specialist centre
- ■ a company location
- ■ rooms hired in a hotel.

You will meet and work with other candidates and may be required to stay overnight. There are also likely to be a number of different recruitment staff and interviewers – some from the company, HR staff and recruitment professionals.

In terms of preparation, it is worth reviewing Chapter 4 to remind yourself about different interview formats. Also practise a range of selection tests as suggested earlier in this chapter and review the guidelines for giving a presentation.

At assessment centre days it is also worth remembering that:

- some tasks may be unexpected
- you are on display for the whole day
- they can be quite demanding and tiring

Also think carefully about any social events, such as an evening meal, that may be part of the assessment centre process. Remember that your behaviour at these events may also be monitored as part of the recruitment process.

Tips for social events

- Wear smart evening clothes.
- Do not drink too much alcohol.
- Be friendly and sociable.
- Avoid excessive 'party' behaviour.
- Stay alert and focused.

Assessment centre recruitment processes are demanding, but they do enable you to show a variety of skills. They also mean that all of your interviews and tests are done in one place, which can cut down on time and travel.

So ensure that you are well prepared and try to relax as much as possible. A lot of people find that they enjoy the day more than they expected and learn a great deal from the experience.

Next steps

This chapter has looked at a variety of different tasks that you might be asked to do in addition to an interview. These range from giving a presentation to completing a variety of selection tests and attending an assessment centre.

Understanding the key features about each of these approaches can help you to prepare effectively for them. This can help you feel more confident and also improve how well you do in any tests.

There are many other aspects to interview preparation and performance. The next two chapters focus on how to make a good impression and stand out from the crowd.

Checklist: selection tests and assessment centres

	✔
Be aware of different types of selection tests	☐
Check which tests you may be asked to complete	☐
Practise a variety of selection tests	☐
Prepare a presentation carefully and practise it	☐

Prepare for all aspects of assessment centre interviews/tests:

■ different interview formats	☐
■ selection tests	☐
■ giving a presentation.	☐

---

6 AIM TO IMPRESS

Interviewers will take into account lots of different issues when forming an opinion about your suitability for a job.

Some of these will be practical things, such as your qualifications and how well you answer the interviewer's questions. However, they will also be forming a broader view of you as a person.

First impressions are especially critical, because we often form a very quick and powerful opinion about someone when we meet them. Body language signals can also tell an interviewer a lot about you.

Understanding more about these issues is important because you will only meet an interviewer for a short period of time, so it is vital to make the most of every moment to create a good impression.

This chapter will:

- explain why first impressions matter
- look at how to create a great first impression
- consider the importance of body language in interviews
- highlight how to avoid negative body language
- identify ways to develop positive body language.

Why do first impressions matter?

When we meet someone for the first time a lot happens. We take in an enormous amount of information about the other person and often make very quick judgements about them.

All of this takes place during the very first few seconds and minutes of meeting!

Our first impression of a new person may be a positive or negative one. And it may be very accurate, or way off the mark. However, our initial response is often so strong that it can be difficult to change it quickly.

Creating a good initial impression really matters because:

- *if you make a poor first impression* – you have very little time to change the interviewer's mind about you
- *if you make a good first impression* – this creates a positive framework for the remainder of the interview.

First impressions therefore really count at an interview.

However, meeting your interviewer for the first time can also be a particularly anxious moment, so how can you ensure that your interview gets off to a flying start?

First, it is important to understand the key elements that help to create a positive first impression. Then it is helpful to practise some of these before you arrive at your interview.

What makes a 'good' first impression?

There are lots of things that contribute to the type of first impression that we make. And it is the combination of these that leads someone to form an overall impression of you.

Some key factors include:

- ■ facial expression
- ■ how you stand/walk
- ■ what you are wearing

■ your tone of voice
■ how you shake hands.

If you look carefully at this list, you will see that many of these factors are visual and body language clues. These non-verbal messages that we send out can be more powerful than what we actually say. An interviewer may therefore form a quick impression of you even before you speak.

For an interview it is therefore useful to develop a greater awareness of how you appear to other people, and to ensure that you give out positive visual and verbal signals – right from the start of your interview. This is not about being super confident, or loud – which in fact are likely to create a poor first impression. Instead it is about presenting a professional appearance, enthusiasm and an open and friendly personality.

Top tips for creating a good first impression

1. *Stand up straight and tall*
   Why? Having a good posture helps you to look more confident and improves the volume and tone of your voice.
2. *Face the interviewer*
   Why? Standing so that you face the interviewer makes you seem much more approachable and friendly.
3. *Make regular eye contact*
   Why? This establishes an important visual connection with the interviewer.
4. *Shake hands*
   Why? It creates a physical connection with the interviewer and helps you appear confident and in control.
5. *Smile!*
   Why? Offering a genuine smile lifts your face, warms the tone of your voice and helps you to relax.

Remember that wearing the right kind of interview outfit will help to create a good first impression too. So also review the 'What am I going to wear?' guidelines in Chapter 3.

Acting the part

The prospect of trying to appear relaxed and confident at the start of an interview may seem like a very tall order. You may also feel that it is all rather a pretence – having to act confidently, while perhaps feeling quite the opposite inside.

However, acting the part like this can actually help to improve your confidence levels. For example, making yourself stand tall and smile will not only make you appear more confident and relaxed, it can also help you to feel calmer as well. This is because standing tall releases tension in your shoulder and neck muscles; and smiling lifts and then relaxes your face muscles.

So here are a range of exercises to help to create a great first impression at your first interview. Try to practise them regularly as part of your interview preparation, so that you feel comfortable with them on the interview day itself.

EXERCISES

1. Posture

Stand in front of a mirror and check out your general posture. For example, do you always stand up straight? Or do you hunch your shoulders and tend to look down at the ground when you are anxious?

Now try:

- holding up your head
- putting your shoulders back

- straightening your spine
- taking a couple of relaxing breaths.

Now take a look in the mirror to see how that has changed your posture. The aim is not to feel stiff and uncomfortable, but to start to see the difference that good posture can make.

If you practise this regularly, you will find it becomes easier and much more natural. And by being more aware of your posture you can stand tall as you head off to your interview.

2. Eye contact

Some people naturally make good eye contact with others, but for others it can be much more difficult. It can be particularly hard in an interview when you have to meet new people. If this is something you find hard to do, it is well worth practising. Pick an ordinary day and simply try making eye contact with people more often.

They could be:

- friends and family
- teachers, lecturers
- colleagues
- staff in shops, cafés and restaurants
- anyone you are meeting for the first time.

Also check out other people's level of eye contact at the same time – it can really help to see how other people manage this.

Be aware, though, that staring at someone the whole time can actually be very intimidating. So you need to find the right balance in terms of the amount of eye contact you make. You want to aim to glance at someone on a regular basis while you are talking to them. And you will find that this becomes much easier with practice.

3. Shaking hands

There is a real art to shaking hands well and a lot of people are not very good at it. So if this is not something that you would normally do, practise with everyone you can – friends, family and anybody else who is willing to help.

TIP Be prepared for a variety of handshake techniques – from a feeble handshake to a crushing grip!

Aim to shake the other person's hand firmly, as if you really mean it. This conveys a sense of confidence that is very effective. Then let go and drop your arm back by your side. Ask anyone you practise with for feedback, as that can really help to ensure that you are getting your handshake right.

4. Smile

Producing a smile at the start of an interview can feel like one of the most challenging things to do. Particularly as you are aiming for a genuine smile, rather than a false or alarming grin.

Just as with improving your eye contact, however, try this one out with people you meet during the course of an ordinary day.

TIP Even a small smile will be effective and will really help to get your interview off to a good start.

You may also find it helpful to practise in front of the mirror. Notice how smiling really lifts your face and features. It can also help to relax your jaw muscles and lift everybody's mood.

First impressions: a step-by-step guide

It can be very useful to think through every step of your first meeting with an interviewer. You cannot plan exactly what will happen, or what will be said. But you can help yourself feel prepared and more confident by actually visualising a few detailed scenarios beforehand.

So here are some general guidelines and things to think about.

Step 1 Arrive in good time

Arriving late and flustered does not create a good impression. And it can also make it much harder to relax and concentrate during the interview itself.

So aim to arrive at least ten minutes early. This will give you some time to gather your thoughts and feel in control at the start of your interview.

Step 2 Who do you need to impress?

Remember that you need to impress not only the interviewer, but also any other staff that you might meet during the day.

So smile and speak politely with everyone you meet, including the receptionist and anyone who takes you to the interview room or brings refreshments.

Step 3 Walk tall

You may be sitting down in reception when the interviewer comes out to meet you, or another member of staff may take you to the interview room.

Remember to collect any bags or coat, but leave a hand free in order to be able to shake hands. Then as the interviewer approaches you, turn to face them, stand tall and smile!

Step 4 Opening the conversation

It is worth thinking about how your initial conversation with the interviewer might go. And have in mind some possible topics of conversation at this introductions stage too.

Some interviewers may not be very chatty, but others may ask you about things like:

- how your journey went
- if you found the company easily
- the weather!

Your opening conversation might go like this:

Interviewer (shaking hands): Good morning, I'm . . . ., welcome to . . . .

You: Good morning, I'm . . . . (full name). Thank you for inviting me for an interview.

Interviewer: How was your journey?
You: Very straightforward, thank you; the map you sent was very useful.

Interviewer: Please have a seat.
You: Thank you.
Interviewer: Now, let me tell you a bit about the interview . . .

The opening conversation might be very short. However, in that first few moments both the interviewer and you will have formed a very quick first impression of each other. And with some thought and preparation, you can get through these introductions confidently and effectively.

The role of body language in interviews

When we meet and talk to someone we exchange a variety of information about ourselves. Some of this is through our voice and the words that we speak. However, we also give out equally important non-verbal signals, as we saw when considering first impressions earlier in the chapter.

In particular, we all use different types of body language. This is all about the physical gestures that we make. And it includes things like how we sit, or the types of movements we make with our hands.

TIP Your body language can make even more of an impact than what you say.

Often we are unaware of our body language. However, understanding body language signals is really useful because it can:

- tell you a lot about how someone is feeling
- help you to communicate positive messages.

And both of these things can be very useful during an interview. You want to ensure that you are giving out the right body language signals; and you can also pick up on the interviewer's non-verbal signals too.

Getting interview body language right

There are whole books written about body language issues, but here we will focus on those that are most relevant to an interview situation.

For example, there are some types of body language that you want to minimise or avoid during an interview. These include anything that might be:

- distracting
- anxiety symptoms
- defensive.

Instead you want to give out as many positive body language signals as possible. This can be done in a whole variety of ways, for example through:

- the way you sit
- facial expressions
- hand movements.

The following sections look first at negative body language, and then at much more positive signals that it can be useful to use at your interview.

Negative body language

As well as identifying different types of negative body language, it is also important to understand why and when they can arise. This can help you to minimise non-verbal signals that may affect your interview.

Here are some key types of negative body language.

1. Distracting body language

This is any gestures that can cause the interviewer to stop listening to what you are saying. They are often unconscious habits and you may have been doing them for years without noticing. Distracting body language includes:

- fiddling with an earring
- turning a ring on your finger
- flicking your hair back
- fiddling with a button
- winding hair round your finger.

These are gestures that people often make repeatedly in stressful situations such as an interview. They can distract the interviewer – and even become highly irritating after a while.

TIP Avoid body language that distracts the interviewer from listening to you.

Try to be aware of any habits like this that you have – ask friends and family if you are not sure. Try to avoid these gestures during an interview, perhaps by keeping your hands clasped on your lap. If necessary, avoid wearing any jewellery that you are tempted to fiddle with.

2. Anxiety and body language

Some body language arises as a direct result of being stressed and anxious. This can therefore be more likely to happen in an interview situation where you are in the spotlight and under some pressure.

A few nervous gestures may be inevitable, but it is possible to minimise these if you know what to look out for.

TIP Ask somebody who knows you well if they are aware of any anxiety gestures that you make.

Anxiety-related gestures include:

- crossing and uncrossing arms/legs
- foot tapping
- finger tapping
- cracking knuckles
- shifting around in the chair.

As well as signalling your high stress levels, these types of movement can be highly distracting to the interviewer. Sitting comfortably at the start of the interview can help, so see the suggestions on this in the next section.

3. Defensive body language

At an interview you can feel rather powerless and not in control of the situation. Your body can then react to feeling threatened by making a variety of defensive gestures.

Defensive body language includes:

- tightly crossing your arms and/or legs
- putting your hand in front of your mouth when talking
- sitting hunched up
- looking down at the floor.

TIP Become more aware of defensive body language – both your own and other people's.

These types of gesture can make you seem rather distant and unfriendly, which can make it hard for the interviewer to feel that they can get to know you. And they may also be concerned that you would find it difficult to fit into the company.

It is therefore worth trying to avoid this type of body language. Try to substitute it with more positive and relaxed gestures that can help to make you seem more approachable. Some examples are described in the following section.

Positive body language

There are lots of different body language signals that it can be really useful to use at an interview. These can help you to:

- seem more confident and relaxed
- emphasise important points you want to make
- liven up how you present yourself.

1. Are you sitting comfortably?

It may seem rather obvious to suggest that you sit comfortably at your interview. However, sitting properly is important because it can:

- help you focus better on the interviewer and their questions
- convey some positive messages to the interviewer.

So just what should you think about when you are invited to sit down? There are a number of things to look out for, such as taking the time to sit comfortably. You also want to aim to look confident and alert.

Top tips for sitting comfortably

Do:
- sit right back in the chair
- take a few moments to get comfortable
- cross your legs at the ankles, or
- cross one leg comfortably over the other knee
- clasp your hands loosely in your lap
- lean forward occasionally to reply to a question.

Don't:
- perch on the edge of the chair
- grip the sides of the chair
- sit with one ankle on the opposite knee
- clasp your hands behind your head
- lounge back in the chair
- tip the chair back.

If you are feeling very anxious, sitting comfortably can also genuinely help you to relax. So if you find yourself hunched forward in the chair with your hands gripped together, sit back and take a couple of calming breaths.

Before your interview, try sitting in different positions to find what is most comfortable for you. Even try this out in front of a mirror, to check how you look.

2. Facial expressions

Faces reveal a great deal about us and how we feel. At an interview, you want your facial expressions to convey positive signals. And they can do this by adding expression and warmth to your interview conversations.

Some people naturally have very lively and animated faces. However, when you are nervous the muscles in your face can tense up. The effect can then be to make you look rather stern and unapproachable.

TIP Try to make your smile as relaxed as possible – a small and genuine smile will be far more effective than a false grin.

Interviews are serious events, however, so it would not be appropriate to spend your time laughing and joking; but the occasional smile can do wonders to lift and animate anybody's features. This can also help to relieve any tension in the interview room.

So it is fine to smile a few times during your interview. It can help you to relax your facial muscles and it also helps engage the interviewer in listening to what you have to say.

3. Hand signals

Moving your hands a lot – such as fiddling with your hair or jewellery – can be highly distracting during an interview. However, the right kind of gestures can actually be very effective. They can, for example:

- emphasise a point that you are trying to make
- liven up what you are saying
- help you seem more confident and relaxed.

Hand signals to use

1. You might be asked to give three reasons why you want to work for the company – counting these off on your fingers can highlight the points you are trying to make.
2. Clasping your hands loosely in your lap makes you appear relaxed.

Hand signals to avoid

1. Do not point at the interviewer – this can seem very threatening.
2. Avoid jabbing your finger to emphasise a point, because it can be interpreted as an aggressive gesture.

A good way to become more aware of hand signals is to watch anyone who regularly gives talks, such as a teacher, lecturer, colleague or TV presenter.

Only use hand gestures that you feel comfortable with. The idea here is not to use exaggerated or false movements, but to introduce subtle gestures that enhance what you are saying.

'Reading' the interviewer

The interviewer will be picking up body language signals from you, but you will also be able to pick up signals from them. This can help you to understand how the interviewer is responding to you. Some people are much harder to 'read' than others, though, so some interviewers might be very animated, while others appear to give little away.

However, if the interviewer is making some regular eye contact with you this is a good sign that they are focused on you. If their gaze is wandering around the room, you may have to work a little harder to get their attention.

It can also help sometimes to copy or 'mirror' the interviewer. People often do this instinctively anyway and it can connect you more effectively with the other person. For example, if the interviewer smiles, you can smile back.

You can also try nodding while the interviewer is asking you a question, to indicate that you are listening. And then sit forward slightly to keep their attention while you give your answer.

All of this needs to be done very subtly, though, and it must not distract you from the task of answering the interview questions. So practise these techniques beforehand and *only* use them if you feel comfortable doing so.

Next steps

Creating a good first impression and thinking about body language issues are all about being more self-aware. And whilst some types of body language might be personal quirks, other gestures can arise because you are stressed and anxious.

Understanding how you might appear to others at an interview can therefore help you avoid giving out too many negative messages.

It may not be possible to avoid some negative signals, but it is worth trying to include a variety of more positive ones. This will be easier if you observe your own body language carefully and practise positive gestures beforehand.

Checklist: aim to impress

	✔
Understand the importance of first impressions	☐

Practise making a good first impression:

	✔
■ good posture	☐
■ making good eye contact	☐
■ shaking hands	☐
■ smiling	☐
■ opening conversation topics.	☐
Understand negative and positive body language	☐

Practise positive body language:

	✔
■ sitting comfortably	☐
■ hand gestures	☐

---

7 STANDING OUT FROM THE CROWD

When you go for your first interview, one of the most difficult things can be to work out how to convince an employer to offer *you* the job. After all, they are likely to be interviewing several people and somehow you want to stand out from the crowd.

This can seem a really difficult task, though. A lot of people are very uncomfortable with the idea of 'selling' themselves. And you may not even be sure how to go about this, or feel that you lack the confidence to do so.

However, standing out on the day does not involve making a dramatic sales pitch. Instead it is about:

- being clear yourself about what you can offer a company
- communicating this effectively to the interviewer.

Everyone has something useful to offer – from being reliable and hard working, to having some relevant work experience or a useful hobby.

You therefore need to identify your key skills and achievements before the interview. And you should also have a plan about how to convey this information during your interview.

This chapter will:

- help you to stand out for the right reasons
- highlight your key personal qualities, skills and achievements

- explain how to identify your 'unique selling point'
- describe how to communicate key messages effectively.

Standing out for the right reasons

Interviewers often spend a long and busy day meeting a variety of applicants. They usually ask all of them the same set of questions – and often hear some very similar answers.

So how can you stand out on the day? And what does this really mean?

First, you want to stand out for the right reasons. You do *not* want to be remembered as:

- the person who was late
- the interviewee who got the company name wrong
- the applicant who tipped their chair back and fell off.

You therefore want to ensure that you get all of the interview basics right. Which means being well prepared, wearing the right outfit and behaving appropriately.

However, simply ticking these boxes may not actually be enough to get you the job, especially if you are competing against a lot of other good candidates.

Standing out on the day therefore requires something a bit more special. It is about taking active steps to present yourself in the best possible light.

In order to achieve this you need to:

- know yourself and your strong points
- plan to ensure that the interviewer is aware of your key qualities
- present this information in the best possible way.

Identifying key skills, strengths and achievements

If you have been offered an interview, you will already have demonstrated that you have some useful skills, qualifications and experience. You then need to build on this during your interview.

You therefore need to spend time reviewing your key skills, strengths and achievements before the big day. This process will help you to clarify what your strong points are. It will also ensure that you can talk effectively about them.

TIP It is not enough to have described yourself effectively in your job application – you now need a clear strategy to convince the interviewer that they should appoint you.

A useful place to start is to review your strengths in relation to the job that you have applied for. These can include a wide variety of different types of personal qualities, skills and abilities. Some of these will be useful for lots of different jobs; others will be specific to a particular area of work.

The following exercises will help you identify these and draw up your own personal list. This will include identifying your top three personal qualities and skills.

You will also need to be able to talk about and illustrate these with practical examples. So these exercises will ask you to think about times when you have developed and used your key skills.

Once you have completed these exercises, the rest of the chapter will help you plan how to use this information during your interview.

1. Personal qualities

Some personal qualities, such as being hard working, are important for any job; so you can take these characteristics for granted and not consider highlighting them at your interview.

However, most companies will have some experience of an employee who regularly turns up late at work, or who needs constant supervision to ensure that they get a job done.

So do not underestimate how valuable personal qualities such as punctuality and reliability can be to a company. Reassuring an interviewer that you are reliable and trustworthy, for example, can be very important and effective.

Simply *saying* this will not be enough, though: you need to be able to offer genuine examples of times when you have displayed these qualities.

EXERCISE 1 IDENTIFY YOUR KEY PERSONAL QUALITIES

Work through the following steps to identify your own key personal qualities:

Step 1
Begin by taking a look through the following list and ticking the qualities that best apply to you. Also add any other qualities that are especially relevant to you.

Personal quality:

determined	☐
hard working	☐
reliable	☐
organised	☐

enthusiastic ☐
quick learner ☐
flexible ☐
self-motivated ☐
proactive ☐
others (add your own)

☐
_____ ☐
_____ ☐
_____

Step 2

Show someone else the list – family member, friend or colleague – and ask how they would describe you.

Does their list match yours? If not, talk about your choices and discuss any differences.

Step 3

Now look through the list of personal qualities again and think about the job that you have applied for.

If you were the interviewer, which of these qualities do you think would be the most important?

Step 4

Now pick three personal qualities that you consider both:

■ describe you best
and
■ are relevant to the job that you have applied for.

Step 5

Think about an example of when you have demonstrated each of these qualities, and what you achieved as a result.

EXAMPLE EXERCISE 1

Personal quality: quick learner.

Example: I helped out with the lighting for our school show earlier this year. During the final week of rehearsals the person in charge of managing the lights was unwell, so I had to take over at the last minute. Although I knew the basics, I had just a couple of days to learn the details of the lighting schemes for every scene in the whole show. I spent some extra time practising with the lighting system too.

Achievement: the show went really well and I was very pleased to have helped make it a success.

2. Skills

Sometimes a job will require particular skills. The company may have identified these in their job advert, job description or person specification. Alternatively you may have highlighted your own particular skill set on your CV.

It is important to review your skill set before your interview. This will help you to be clear about what you can offer the company. It will also enable you to highlight any examples of your skills to the interviewer.

There are different types of skills, such as:

- communication skills – e.g. telephone skills, report writing skills
- people skills – e.g. teamworking skills, leadership skills
- technical skills – e.g. using a till, IT skills.

EXERCISE 2 IDENTIFYING YOUR KEY SKILLS

Work through the following steps to identify your own key skills.

Step 1
Begin by taking a look through the following list and ticking all the skills that best apply to you.

Also add any other skills that are relevant to the job you have applied for.

Skill:

spoken communication e.g. telephone skills ☐
written communication e.g. report writing ☐
numerical ☐
IT ☐
problem solving ☐
teamworking ☐
research ☐
technical/practical e.g. using a till ☐
time management ☐
leadership ☐
customer service ☐
others (add your own)

_____ ☐
_____ ☐
_____ ☐

Step 2
Now remind yourself about the job – what key tasks are involved and which skills are required?

Step 3

Now pick three skills that you consider:

- ■ you can demonstrate best

and

- ■ are relevant to the job that you have applied for.

Step 4

Think about an example of when you have developed and/or demonstrated each of these skills and what you achieved as a result.

EXAMPLE EXERCISE 2

Key skills: research skills

Example: for my brother's 18th birthday earlier this year my family wanted to hold a party for him. We decided to hire somewhere, but we had to stick to a bit of a budget. So I looked in some telephone directories and online to get the contact numbers of some different places. I also asked friends at school for ideas. As a result I found three potential venues that we then visited. This gave us the opportunity to compare the different places and prices.

Achievement: we chose a local community centre hall in the end because it was good value and gave us a lot of flexibility. For example, we could decorate it ourselves and provide refreshments too. So taking the time to do some research definitely helped to find the best option.

3. Unique selling point

When you are preparing for your interview it is important to think about anything that is particularly special about you. This is sometimes known as a unique selling point (USP). It could be something that is different about you, important, interesting, or that you are especially proud of.

Some people find this very difficult – because they worry that they have to come up with something really amazing, different, or exciting.

However, it could be a very down-to-earth and practical thing – such as a project that you did at school or college. Alternatively it could be an interesting hobby, or a trip that you have made. It could even be one of your key personal qualities or skills.

The most important thing is that it is something memorable about *you* – and that you can talk about it in a way that is relevant to the job that you have applied for.

It therefore needs to be something that it would be useful for the employer to know about. And that could help you to stand out from the crowd. You do not have to refer to it in the interview as your USP – but you should certainly be clear yourself that it is something to be proud of.

EXERCISE 3 IDENTIFYING YOUR USP

Work through the following steps to identify your own USP.

Step 1
Begin by looking through the following list to start you thinking about USP ideas.

- School/college project.
- Saturday job.
- Work experience.
- Problem that you have solved or overcome.

- Trip, journey, holiday.
- Hobby/interest.
- Responsibility – at school, home, work.
- Achievement that you are proud of.
- Personal quality or skill (see Exercises 1 and 2).
- Unusual mix of skills/qualifications/experience.

Try to think of two or three different ideas. If you find this difficult, talk to somebody who knows you. Another person's input can offer a different perspective and help to spark off some ideas.

Step 2

Now pick out one key USP idea and think about:

- how to describe it in one sentence
- why it is important to you
- why it might be relevant to the job that you have applied for.

Step 3

Think about an example of when you have developed and/or demonstrated your USP and what you achieved as a result.

EXAMPLE EXERCISE 3

USP: I can offer a mix of creative skills and IT skills.

Example: I have helped to edit our school magazine for the past couple of years. This requires a variety of skills, but I particularly like sorting out the layout of the magazine. It is really important to make the pages look as interesting and attractive as possible. This is a very creative task, but it also requires good IT skills to arrange the layout on the computer.

Achievement: the readership of the school magazine has increased over the past two years. This is thanks to a big team effort, but we have had very good feedback about the new look and layout of the magazine.

Planning to 'sell' yourself

At an interview, you are aiming to present yourself in the best possible light. This is not about boasting or giving misleading information. It is about conveying to the interviewer the most important and relevant facts about you.

You only have a short amount of time at an interview, so you need to avoid being too modest and instead promote your strong points. The earlier exercises in this chapter will have helped you to identify these.

You now need to plan how to communicate this information to the interviewer.

You can do this in a number of ways, including:

■ providing relevant highlights about yourself
■ using different stages of the interviews effectively
■ using positive and upbeat language.

1. Providing relevant information

It is helpful before an interview to focus on preparing for the questions an interviewer might ask you. However, it is equally important to identify what key information you want to convey to the interviewer. In particular, do not assume that the interviewer will know everything about you. They should have read your job application carefully, but during a busy day of interviewing they might overlook an important fact in your written application.

The interview questions should give you the opportunity to talk about things like your personal qualities, skills and achievements, but you also need to be prepared to bring these issues up yourself. So you need to be proactive and decide beforehand what facts you want to ensure the interviewer knows about you. It can help to think of these as 'news headlines' about yourself.

Before your interview, identify and review:

- your list of top three personal qualities and examples
- your list of top three skills and examples
- your USP and examples.

You need to ensure that you can talk fluently and convincingly about these. And this means having clear and effective examples to back up your claims.

As well as highlighting information from your job application, also think about anything else that it might be useful to raise. In particular, do demonstrate that you are well prepared for the interview.

TIP Tell the interviewer that you have taken the time to research the job or company – mention that you have looked at the company website, know about a new product launch, or have talked to somebody who works there.

If you are asked a question about the job or company, for example, plan to mention in your answer that you have done some research. This will help to support any claims that you make about yourself that you are organised, take the initiative or use your research skills.

2. Using different stages of the interview effectively

When planning how to convey your key messages, you need to think in advance how to bring these up at different stages of the interview. It can help to think about three different stages of your interview.

Stage 1 Start

At the beginning of your interview, you might be asked some open-ended, icebreaker questions, for example, 'Tell me about yourself/your CV.'

You can use this type of question to flag up some key 'news headlines' about yourself. So highlight the key skills that you can offer, or a relevant personal quality. You could also briefly talk about your USP and how it relates to the job.

This will mean that the interviewer is aware early on about some of your key qualities and skills. They can then ask you about them in more detail during the rest of the interview.

Stage 2 Main questions

Always make the most of any open-ended questions during the central part of your interview. Use these to highlight your key personal qualities and skills. And give specific examples of when you have developed and used them.

Stage 3 Ending

Towards the end of the interview you are likely to be given the opportunity to ask questions. This can also be an opportunity to offer any additional information about yourself.

Avoid repeating information that you have given during the interview. However, you may feel that there is a key skill that you have not had the opportunity to talk about. If you have forgotten to mention something relevant, you could also raise it at this stage. For example:

- 'I would also like to add that . . .'
- 'I must mention that . . .'
- 'One final point that I would like to highlight . . .'

3. Using positive and upbeat language

There are different types of language that you can use to talk about yourself at an interview. The key aim is to use lots of words and phrases that are positive and upbeat. You also want to avoid using any negative or apologetic language.

Using positive language can convey much more energy and enthusiasm in what you say. This will help to emphasise your key messages to the interviewer. And make you much more interesting to listen to.

Positive language

Do say:
- 'I really love . . .'
- 'I have some very relevant experience . . .'
- 'I am particularly good at . . .'
- 'I always enjoy . . .'
- 'I am especially interested . . .'
- 'I have covered all the main points . . .'

Don't say:
- 'I quite like . . .'
- 'I have only got a bit of work experience . . .'
- 'I am not much good at . . .'
- 'I sometimes enjoy . . .'
- 'I am fairly interested in . . .'
- 'I can't think of anything else . . .'

Also aim to end your interview conversations on an upbeat final point. Even if you have started an answer positively, for example, ending rather half-heartedly can leave a poor impression. So plan and practise interview answers that use positive words and phrases throughout.

Next steps

It is important to actively plan what information you want the interviewer to know about you. This type of preparation can ensure that you do not forget anything vital. It can also help you to identify and talk effectively about your strong points.

Spending time identifying things like your key personal qualities, skills and USP is therefore very useful. It is also a good way to help you feel more confident before your interview and ensure that you do yourself justice at your interview.

Checklist: standing out from the crowd

✔

Identify your top three personal qualities ☐

Identify your top three skills ☐

Identify your USP ☐

Draw up some 'news headlines' about yourself ☐

Practise using positive and upbeat language ☐

---

8 FACING YOUR FEARS

Most people feel a bit anxious before an interview. You may be concerned, however, that your nerves are going to affect how you come across at your interview.

If this is the case, it is worth setting aside some time to manage your stress levels. Generally feeling well prepared can make a big difference to your confidence levels. So allowing yourself as much time as possible for interview planning and preparation can really help.

It can also be useful to understand more about anxiety and its symptoms. This can help you to develop coping strategies – both before and during your interview.

This chapter will:

■ explain what causes anxiety
■ describe the symptoms of anxiety
■ help you to identify your own anxiety triggers
■ offer tips on mental preparation
■ identify relaxation techniques.

What makes us feel anxious?

Some situations can make you feel more anxious than others. Sitting at home watching your favourite TV programme is unlikely to raise your stress levels very far. However, the thought of being in the spotlight at an interview can be very scary indeed.

The types of situations where you might find yourself feeling anxious can include:

- being tested (e.g. an exam, a driving test)
- giving a public performance (e.g. a presentation, a show)
- undertaking something risky (e.g. a rollercoaster ride, parachute jump)
- doing something for the first time (e.g. starting college, a new job).

Your first job interview is an experience that contains elements of all of these, so it would be strange if you did not feel a bit anxious. It is therefore understandable and normal to feel nervous in an interview situation.

The symptoms of anxiety

One of our most basic human responses occurs when we feel threatened, or find ourselves in a stressful situation.

Our body reacts by producing a chemical called adrenalin. And there can be some real benefits to your adrenalin levels shooting up: it can improve your mental and physical performance levels, helping you to think more quickly, or run faster.

So feeling a bit anxious about your interview can actually be a good thing. For example, your raised adrenalin levels might improve your reaction times to questions.

However, very high stress levels can sometimes get in the way of performing well at an interview. Some of the physical symptoms can include things like:

- faster heart rate
- sweating
- flushing
- dry mouth
- feeling shaky

- tense muscles
- feeling panicky.

Sometimes these anxiety symptoms can make it harder to focus during the interview, so it might feel difficult to remember things, or to find the right words. It can also be hard to hide some of these symptoms, which can make you feel even more anxious.

TIP Remember that interviewers will understand if you are a bit nervous about your interview.

It is therefore useful to control and manage your stress levels both before and during your interview. There are lots of different ways to do this, including doing the right mental preparation. You can also use relaxation techniques both before and during your interview. These are described later in this chapter, but first you need to assess your own individual anxiety levels.

Individual anxiety levels

Different people feel anxious and stressed about different things. A rollercoaster ride might be one person's idea of a real treat; but it might be someone else's worst nightmare.

Similarly, everyone reacts differently to an interview situation. Your stress response will also depend on the sort of person you are. Some people rarely get anxious about anything; others worry about lots of things.

Just the thought of an interview might be enough to set your stress levels soaring. You could feel:

- a general sense of panic
- worried about having to talk about yourself
- concern about getting something wrong.

Sometimes a particular interview task might be the problem. You may feel reasonably confident about a face-to-face interview, but would lose sleep if you also had to give a presentation.

How anxious are you?

In order to understand more about your own feelings about your interview, try answering the following questions.

1. How anxious do you feel about each of these?

	Low				High
Your interview	1	2	3	4	5
What to wear	1	2	3	4	5
Finding the interview location	1	2	3	4	5
Making a good first impression	1	2	3	4	5
Answering questions	1	2	3	4	5
Asking questions	1	2	3	4	5
Talking confidently about yourself	1	2	3	4	5
Doing some selection tests	1	2	3	4	5
Giving a presentation	1	2	3	4	5

2. Is there anything else you are worried about?

....

....

....

....

Your answers to these questions will help you to start to pin down just how nervous you feel. They will also help you to identify exactly what is causing you the most concern. This can be useful, as you can then start to plan how to best to manage any anxieties that you have.

TIP Being well prepared for your interview is one of the best ways of reducing your anxiety levels and help you feel more confident.

So do any practical preparation that will help you deal with a specific anxiety. If you are most concerned about giving a presentation, for example, give this task as much time and practice as possible.

Two other important methods involve doing some mental preparation and relaxation exercises. Mental preparation is all about getting into a positive mindset, and relaxation techniques can help you feel calmer and manage your stress levels.

Mental preparation

A lot of interview preparation is about doing practical things such as making lists, getting an outfit ready and practising questions.

However, mental preparation can be just as important – particularly if you are feeling anxious. This is because it can help you develop a more positive and confident approach to your interview.

There are a variety of different types of mental preparation. Try out the following and see which work best for you.

- Positive thinking.
- Being prepared.
- Dealing with disaster.
- Developing self-belief.
- Talking to someone.

1. Positive thinking

How you think about a task can make a lot of difference to how well you do it. If you feel positive about doing something, you are more likely to enjoy it and carry it out effectively.

It is also possible to get into a negative spiral of thoughts. This is when one smaller anxiety can quickly set off other more serious concerns. Here are some examples of negative thinking.

- You start off being anxious about a particular question that you might be asked.
- You go on to worry that you will be unable to answer any question.
- You end up convincing yourself that the entire interview is going to be a disaster . . .

However, it is possible to break this chain of negative thinking. The aim is to keep overriding negative thoughts with more

Quit negative thinking

Quit the negative thought.
U-turn your thinking.
Introduce a positive thought.
Transform your thinking through practice.

Example 1

Negative thought: 'I'm going to do really badly at my interview.'
Positive alternative: 'If I am well prepared I will be able to really do myself credit.'

Example 2

Negative thought: 'I'm bound not to be able to answer any questions.'
Positive alternative: 'I'll be able to deal with most questions if I practise.'

Example 3

Negative thought: 'Everyone else will be better than me.'
Positive alternative: 'I have a lot of good personal qualities and skills to offer.'

positive ones. This can help to distract you and avoid your thoughts spiralling out of control.

Negative thinking can become a bit of a habit, especially if you are rather stressed. So try to avoid it by practising this QUIT exercise in the run-up to your interview.

2. Being prepared

If you are feeling anxious, it can be tempting to avoid doing anything related to interview preparation. However, it is worth channelling some of your energies into being well prepared as soon as you hear that you have an interview.

This can help to:

- improve your confidence levels
- reduce your stress levels
- increase your chances of doing well.

So allow plenty of time to do some preparation and make a detailed plan to make good use of any time. In particular,

Example 1

If you worried about answering a question concerning your exam grades, for example, work on your answer to this one first. Then move on to a wider range of questions, but come back to this question regularly until you are comfortable with your answer.

Example 2

If you are concerned about having to do some selection tests, begin by organising this area of preparation first. Buy or borrow a book of tests, or look some up online. Then practise a variety of tests regularly – and set yourself time limits so that you get used to managing your time.

focus on those things that you are most concerned about and make them a priority in your planning.

Refer back to Chapters 2 and 3 to help you identify how to prepare effectively for your interview.

3. Dealing with disaster

Another way to manage your anxieties can be to deal with them head on. This means thinking about the most disastrous thing that might happen at your interview. You can then plan how you would deal with it.

TIP Confronting your worst fears can actually help you to get them into perspective.

Example 1

'I am really worried that my mind will go blank during the interview.'

If this happens: there will be a long pause and I will feel embarrassed.

How to manage the situation: I can simply be honest and explain to the interviewer what has happened. I can take a deep breath, ask them to repeat the question and have a go at answering if possible. Then we can move on to the next question.

Example 2

'I'm certain that they won't offer me the job.'

If this happens: I am going to feel really disappointed and upset.

How to manage the situation: I need to have a back-up plan, such as having other job applications under way. And I will learn a lot from my interview experience and can use this in the future.

This may sound rather a negative approach, but it can prevent a worry from building up to be a big issue in your mind.

The best way to do this is to write down what is worrying you. This will help you to pin down exactly what your main concerns are. Then try picturing in your mind what might happen next and think about how to manage the situation.

4. Developing self-belief

Identifying things like your key personal qualities and skills is only one half of preparing for an interview. You also need to believe in yourself and your ability to do the job.

For example, you might plan to say that you are a determined person. However, you also have to sound as though you really believe it – otherwise the interviewer is unlikely to be convinced.

One way of improving your confidence and developing self-belief is to think of examples of your key achievements. Keep reminding yourself of these, because they are genuine evidence to support your claims.

It can also help to practise your interview skills in front of a mirror, or to video yourself. Most people are surprised at how convincing they can be, in spite of feeling anxious. It can also be useful to repeat a confidence-boosting phrase regularly to yourself.

EXERCISE 1 INTERVIEW QUESTIONS AND PRESENTATIONS

Try practising by speaking out loud:

- in front of a mirror
- while videoing yourself, e.g. on a mobile phone.

EXERCISE 2 POSITIVE TALKING

Think of a phrase to boost your confidence and practise saying it regularly:

- in your mind
- in front of a mirror.

For example:

- 'I can do this job.'
- 'I have all the right skills.'
- 'I am proud of my achievements.'

5. Talking to someone

Sharing your anxieties with someone is a good way of getting things into perspective. Simply telling someone that you are worrying about your interview can significantly reduce your stress levels.

It can also be easy to underestimate your abilities and skill set. Someone else can often give you a different and much more positive view of yourself. So it can really help to talk about any concerns with a friend, relation or careers adviser.

And do remember that interviewers will understand that you may be anxious. They will take this into account and will do their best to help you feel comfortable on the day.

Relaxation techniques

Anxiety can cause a variety of symptoms, but relaxation techniques can help to counteract these. They can help you to feel less stressed and calmer. They can therefore be useful both in the run-up to your interview and on the day itself.

To be effective, relaxation techniques do require practice. So it is worth including some in your planning schedule and using them regularly.

There are a variety of different types of relaxation techniques. Try these out and see which ones work best for you:

- exercise
- breathing techniques
- muscle relaxation
- visualisation.

1. Exercise

When our bodies produce adrenalin, it can improve our performance levels in the short term. It can help us, for example, to run faster.

So one very practical way of managing your stress levels can be to do exercise. This can be anything from walking to swimming or jogging. It could also include playing a game of football, dancing and even singing.

TIP Even going for a short walk can help you to feel calmer and more relaxed.

Doing some exercise like this can reduce adrenalin levels, help you to breathe more deeply and relax your muscles. It can even boost levels of chemicals in the body that improve your mood.

Instead of sitting fretting about an interview, getting out and doing some exercise can therefore help to reduce anxiety levels. It can also put you in a better mood for doing some interview preparation, or even for the interview itself.

Using exercise

Example 1

Plan to do some regular exercise in the run-up to your interview. This could be going to the gym, swimming, or any sport that you enjoy.

Example 2

If you arrive at your interview location in good time, go for a quick walk around the block first. This can help to relax you a bit before your interview gets under way.

2. Breathing techniques

When you get anxious, you can find yourself breathing much too quickly. So another relaxation technique involves taking some slow, deep and calming breaths.

To steady your breathing, try breathing in through your nose and out through your mouth. Also try counting as you breathe in and out. Start by counting to three each time – then build up to a count of five, or whatever feels comfortable.

This technique can help you to feel calmer very quickly, so it is a useful one to use while you are waiting for your interview.

And if you feel anxious during the interview itself, try taking one or two slower breaths to relax yourself.

3. Muscle relaxation

It is very common to tense your muscles up when you are feeling anxious. Many people tense up muscles in particular parts of their body, for example hunching up your shoulders or clenching your hands.

As part of your interview preparation you could try doing a muscle relaxation exercise. This can help you to identify which muscles you tend to tense up. It can also help to make you feel much calmer.

RELAXATION EXERCISE

1. Sit or lie down somewhere comfortably.
2. Take a few deep breaths.
3. Tense up and then relax the muscles in one foot.
4. Then do the same with your other foot.
5. Gradually work up your body to your face.
   - Right foot, left foot.
   - Right leg, left leg.
   - Stomach.
   - Chest.
   - Back.
   - Right hand, left hand.
   - Right arm, left arm.
   - Neck and shoulders.
   - Face.
6. Take a few final relaxing breaths.

On the day of the interview itself, try tensing and relaxing specific muscles. Focus on your hands, for example, if you tend to clench them into fists.

Also remember to smile! This can really help you to relax your facial muscles, as well as making you seem much more friendly and approachable.

4. Visualisation

Another way to relax involves distracting yourself from any anxieties and stressful feelings. The idea is to imagine a situation where you feel happy and relaxed. This might be a holiday location that you can remember, or a calm room at home. It could be your garden, or an imaginary scene.

VISUALISATION EXERCISE

1. Sit or lie down somewhere comfortably.
2. Take a few deep breaths.
3. Picture your ideal situation as clearly as possible.
4. Think about what you can see, hear, smell and feel there.
5. Let your worries drift away.
6. Take a few final deep breaths.

Try this visualisation exercise regularly before your interview, in order to get used to the process. You can also use it on your interview day. For example, take a few minutes to do the exercise before you set out to the interview.

Next steps

Feeling anxious is natural and understandable before an interview. And most interviewers will be aware of this and try to put you at your ease.

However, it can be useful to actively plan to manage your stress levels. The mental preparation exercises and relaxation techniques described here are all simple, but very effective. So build them into your interview preparation and practise them regularly to see which ones work best for you.

Checklist: facing your fears

✔

Make a detailed plan and allow plenty of preparation time ☐

Identify your main areas of concern ☐

Talk to someone about your concerns ☐

Practise mental preparation exercises ☐

Practise relaxation techniques ☐

---

9 QUESTIONS, QUESTIONS AND MORE QUESTIONS!

Interview questions are usually one of everybody's key concerns. This is because you don't know exactly what the interviewer will ask you. And of course you also have to come up with an answer straightaway – there is no option to phone a friend!

You may be wondering about things like this:

- What is the interviewer going to ask?
- What is the best way to answer a question?
- What should I do if I don't know the answer?

It is certainly worth spending some time understanding and thinking about interview questions. This will help you to be well prepared to deal with a wide variety of different topics and types of question.

This does not mean learning answers off by heart though. Instead, it is about ensuring that you have the right information in your mind to draw on at the interview. It is also important to understand how to give clear, relevant and concise answers.

This chapter will:

- explain how to answer questions effectively
- identify different types of interview question
- help you to deal with tricky questions
- identify questions you can ask
- describe how to practise interview questions.

How to answer questions effectively

Whatever questions you are asked at your interview, there are some useful basic guidelines to providing good answers.

The most important of these is to make sure that you:

Answer the question!

This sounds obvious, but do listen carefully to each question. It can be easy to pick up on one key word, rather than listening to the whole question. This is especially the case if you are a bit nervous, when the temptation can be to rush into answering.

Which question?

An interviewer asks you a question about 'skills'.

They may be asking for:

- a summary of your skill set, e.g. 'Can you highlight your key skills for me?'
- more details about one particular skill, e.g. 'Tell me more about your teamworking skills.'
- an example of an occasion when you developed or used a skill, e.g. 'Can you give me an example of when you used time management skills?'

You cannot give a good answer if you have not understood the question. So if you are really not sure what a question means, do ask for it to be repeated, or explained.

There are also different *ways* of asking questions. It can be useful to recognise these, as it can help you understand the kind of answer that is needed.

Some key questioning styles include the following.

1. Closed questions

These could be answered with just a 'Yes' or 'No' – or any simple, one-word answer. Most interviewers avoid them, because they don't encourage a detailed answer.

How to deal with them

Offer a bit more information to expand on your answer. You could explain why you like something, or describe a specific aspect that interests you.

Example: closed question

Q: What is your favourite GCSE subject?
A: I really enjoy history. I particularly love modern history and understanding how it has influenced our lives today.

With this example you could just have answered, 'History', but this more detailed answer is far more interesting and thoughtful.

2. Open questions

Open questions require more than a one-word answer. They are questions which ask you to describe or explain something.

They can be very general questions, such as these.

- ■ Tell me a bit about . . .   yourself
                                your work experience
                                a hobby
- ■ Explain why you . . .   chose this subject/course
                                want to work for us

How to deal with them

The key here is to give a concise and structured answer. So take your time, aim to make three or four key points and speak for about a minute.

Example: open question

Q: Tell me a bit about your work experience.

A: I spent two weeks working at a local estate agent. I did a variety of work including filing, photocopying and answering the telephone. This all helped to develop my administrative skills and I really enjoyed being part of such a hard-working and friendly team of people.

This example describes for the interviewer what the work was about. It also usefully highlights the skills gained and the valuable teamworking experience. This avoids waffling and provides a focused and relevant answer instead.

3. Competency questions

The interviewer will ask you to give an example of a time when you demonstrated a skill or carried out a task. The question will usually relate to the job you have applied for, and it might be about:

- solving a problem
- dealing with lots of deadlines
- showing some initiative.

How to deal with them

Make sure that you describe a relevant and specific event. It might be to do with your studies, work experience or interests.

In this example the answer begins by explaining the problem clearly and then describing a successful solution. In this case

Example: competency question

Q: **Tell me about a time when you had to deal with lots of deadlines.**

A: Last summer I had to manage a lot of different study deadlines, as well as my regular Saturday job. So I sat down and wrote out a timetable for my essay deadlines, projects and revision. I also decided to cut back a bit on seeing friends for a few weeks. And as a result, I managed to get everything done on time.

it also demonstrates the ability to prioritise and schedule both study and work commitments.

Use real examples and have some in mind before your interview. You can think about these when you review your job application and any details you have about the job. If a job requires a variety of skills, for example, then think of occasions when you have demonstrated each of these skills.

4. Situational questions

If you are asked a situational question, the interviewer will describe a situation to you and ask you how you might respond. Often it will be a tricky or difficult scenario that might occur if you were doing the job.

This type of question might start with phrases like:

- What would you do if . . . ?
- Describe how you might deal with . . .
- How would you handle a problem such as . . . ?

How to deal with them

Describe the steps that you would take to deal with the situation. And explain why you would handle something in that particular way too.

Example: situational question

Q: Describe how you would deal with a customer who is angry because they have bought a faulty product from the shop.

A: I would listen carefully to the customer to start with, to make sure that I understood the problem. I think it would also be important for me to be polite and stay calm at this stage, to avoid aggravating the situation. Then I would explain that I would like to help them and will need some further information – such as when they bought the product and if they had a receipt. And then I would describe any options available to them, such as replacing the product or having it repaired.

Recognising a situational question will enable you to answer it much more clearly and effectively. Take your time to think through your answer, rather than rushing in. And if you have ever managed a similar situation successfully, mention this in your answer.

Top tips on interview questions and answers

Do:
- listen carefully to the question
- take your time considering your answer
- think about how to structure your answer
- aim to make three or four key points
- give relevant information
- have a clear ending to your answer.

Don't:
- rush into giving your answer
- only answer part of the question
- give a single-word answer
- talk about things that are not relevant
- waffle on endlessly.

Different interview question topics

Most interview questions fall into one of a number of different subject categories. So you may not be able to predict precisely what questions the interviewer will ask. However, you can think about and prepare for questions about specific topics.

Some key areas of questions include:

- icebreaker topics
- education and qualifications
- skills and experience
- the job
- the company
- your personality
- your achievements and ambitions
- your hobbies and interests.

Interview questions may therefore be concerned with the sort of person you are, your skills and experience. Other questions may focus on the job itself, the company and its products and services.

1. Icebreaker questions

These are introductory questions that you may be asked at the start of an interview. Often the interviewer will ask them in order to help you relax a bit.

However, you should always take these questions seriously. They set the scene for the rest of your answers and so it is worth being prepared for them.

Sometimes the interviewer will begin by asking questions about your journey – particularly if you have travelled some distance. And if you have stayed overnight, they may ask you about your accommodation.

The interviewer may also begin with a few comments about something newsworthy. This could be anything from a political event to unseasonal weather!

Tips for answering icebreaker questions

1. Be upbeat – do not dwell too much on any negative aspects of your journey.
2. Avoid criticism – try not to pick fault with any arrangements made by the company.
3. Do not waffle – keep answers informative and reasonably short.

Your aim in answering icebreaker questions is to get the interview off to as good a start as possible. So now is not the moment to dwell on any bad news. Instead keep things positive and upbeat.

2. Education and qualifications

Your main qualifications are likely to have been listed on your application, but the interviewer may want to know more about them, especially if you do not have much work experience.

These are some potential questions about your studies.

- Why did you choose this particular subject/college/location?
- What are your favourite subject(s)?
- Tell me about your grades.
- Tell me about your project/field trips/practical work.

TIP Always be prepared for some questions about your choice of studies and qualifications.

You may be also be asked questions which relate to the job itself.

- How are your qualifications relevant to this job?
- What further training do you think you might need?
- How will you cope with both work and study?

It is therefore well worth spending some time looking through your educational history. Think about which subjects and qualifications might interest the interviewer. Also consider any questions that you might be asked about further training if this is relevant to the job you have applied for.

3. Skills and experience

The interviewer will want to understand the range of skills that you can offer. They will also be interested in learning more about any work experience you have done. Any questions about skills are likely to be related to the job you have applied for.

Here are some potential questions about your skills.

- What are your key skills?
- Tell me how you developed this skill.
- Can you give an example of when you used this particular skill?

TIP Review your job application and any job details to remind yourself of the key skills required.

Also be prepared for questions regarding any work experience.

- What type of work experience have you done?
- What were your key tasks/responsibilities?
- How would this experience help with the job you have applied for?

129

- What did you enjoy/dislike about your work experience?
- What are the key things you learned from your work experience?
- Did you have to deal with any challenges during your work experience?

Before your interview, aim to be clear about the key skills that you can offer the company. Also think carefully about any work experience that you have done. In particular, consider how this might help you to do the job that you are being interviewed for.

4. The job

The interviewer is going to want to know that you understand what the job is about. They will not expect you to know every detail, but will want to be reassured that you are aware of the main tasks. They may also be interested in understanding why you want to do this type of work.

These are some potential questions about the job.

- Why have you applied for this job?
- What do you think the job involves?
- Why are you interested in doing this sort of work?

An interviewer may want to know if you are prepared to work particular hours, shifts or at weekends. They may also want you to work on a trial basis to begin with, or on a temporary contract.

TIP For further information about checking and negotiating the details of a job offer, see Chapter 12.

These are some possible additional questions about work arrangements.

- How do you feel about working on a trial basis?
- Would you be prepared to work on a temporary contract?
- What hours/days/shifts could you work?

It is therefore useful to be prepared for these questions. Think in advance about any possible working arrangements and what you may be able to commit to. Also check that anything that you agree with the interviewer is confirmed in writing when you are offered the job.

5. The company

Lots of different companies offer similar types of work. You may even have applied for the same job with a variety of different organisations. So the interviewer is going to want to know why you want to work for them in particular.

Here are some potential questions about the company.

- Why do you want to work for us?
- Do you know what our company does?
- What can you tell me about out key products/services?
- How big do you think the company is? (staff numbers, turnover, etc.)
- What are the company's key departments/locations?

You could also be asked some more detailed questions about a new company project. Other questions may be concerned with broader questions about the industry or sector.

TIP Always check whether a company has a website, as this can be a very quick way to find out some useful information.

More detailed questions about the company could include these.

- What do you know about this new product/service?
- What did you think about the recent news about our company?
- What threats/opportunities does this industry/sector face?
- Who do you think are our main competitors?

So always try and do some research about the company beforehand. Even a small company is likely to have a website, or produce some publicity leaflets. Being familiar with these can really help to underline your commitment to working for them.

6. Your personality

As well as knowing about your skills and experience, interviewers may also want to know more about the sort of person you are. You may therefore be asked to describe your personal qualities, which can include things like being:

- reliable
- hard working
- good at thinking up new ideas
- organised
- adaptable
- up for a challenge.

In particular, an interviewer will be looking for personal qualities that will help you to do the job they are offering. So try to think which of your qualities will be most relevant to that specific role. Also check if any are identified in any information that you have about the job.

TIP Ask somebody who knows you well – a friend, family, teacher – to help identify your best personal qualities.

An interviewer may also want to understand how you will fit into their company and work with colleagues. You may therefore be asked questions about how you get on with other people and teamworking skills.

Here are some questions about your ability to get on with people.

- What contribution could you make to the team?
- Can you give me an example of when you showed leadership skills?
- How might a friend or colleague describe you?
- Have you ever had problems getting on with someone?

Think about examples of times when you have displayed specific personal qualities. This will enable you able to back up your claims and sound convincing.

7. Your achievements and ambitions

You may be asked some questions about your achievements so far in life. These could be about anything relating to your studies, work experience or interests.

Here are some potential questions about achievements.

- Can you describe a key achievement that you are proud of?
- Tell me about a time when you made a difference.

Try to think about specific examples of occasions when you have achieved something. This could be something like organising an event, or learning a new skill. It could also be something simple such as completing a project on time.

The important thing is to be able to describe what you did, any problems you overcame and how you managed this. Also take the opportunity to highlight any skills that will be relevant to the job.

An interviewer may also be interested in your future goals and ambitions. They will be trying to understand your future plans and how these might fit with their company.

You could be asked the following questions about your ambitions.

- What are your career goals?
- Where do you see yourself in a few years' time?

Try to describe career ambitions that you might achieve with this particular company. The aim is to show that you have a career plan. However, the company will also be hoping that you will be committed to staying with them for some time too.

8. Your hobbies and interests

A company may also want to hear more about how you spend your spare time. This can tell them more about you as a person, particularly at the start of your career when you may not have much work experience.

These are some potential questions about hobbies and interests.

- What is your favourite hobby?
- What led you to choose this particular interest?
- What do you enjoy about this hobby?
- What have you learnt through your interests?
- How would this interest be relevant to the job?

It is worth giving some thought to which hobbies and interests you list on your application. Avoid general things that everyone does – such as watching TV, or listening to music. Instead, highlight anything that would be interesting and relevant to talk about.

Tricky interview questions

Some interview questions can be more difficult to answer than others. It may be that the question itself is not clear, or that you simply do not know the answer.

Thinking about how to deal with these situations beforehand can be useful. This can help you handle difficult questions more effectively during the interview itself.

Tricky interview questions include:

- multiple questions
- negative questions
- questions you cannot answer
- questions that worry you.

1. Multiple questions

Most experienced interviewers will ask you some clear and relevant questions. However, sometimes you might find yourself faced with several questions all at once. For example: 'Tell me a bit about your qualifications and also why you chose to study at this particular university. And what you most enjoyed about the course.'

This type of questioning can be pretty confusing. It can be very hard to remember all the questions. You may also not be sure which one to answer first.

So stay calm if you are asked any type of multiple question. It is fine to ask the interviewer for some clarification if you find yourself faced with this kind of questioning. Then work through each question in turn and keep your answers clear and concise.

Top tips for answering a multiple question

1. Ask the interviewer to repeat the questions if necessary.
2. Answer the first question – and then ask them to repeat the remaining questions.
3. Deal with the questions one at a time.

2. Negative questions

Some questions are specially designed to tempt you into giving negative answers. They try to make you focus on things such as weaknesses, or occasions when things have gone wrong. Here are some examples.

- ■ 'What are your weaknesses?'
- ■ 'Tell me about a time when you did not achieve your goals.'
- ■ 'Have you ever made a mistake?'

These questions invite you to highlight things that present you in a poor light. However, once you learn to recognise them, you can always turn this type of question around.

Top tips for answering a negative question

- Explain how you overcame a problem.
- Describe what you learned from a difficult situation.
- Highlight how you would go about doing something differently.

Nobody's perfect, so it can be easy to get drawn into discussing times when things have gone wrong. Aim to shift the focus away from more negative issues. Instead move on to empha-sise your positive qualities, or what you have learnt from deal-ing with a problem.

3. Questions you cannot answer

If you are well prepared for an interview, you will be able to answer most types of question. However, you may occasionally be unsure how to answer a particular question. Or your mind might simply go blank.

If this does happen, do not pretend to know the answer, or waffle. Instead, ask for the question to be repeated if this would be helpful. And then try to make some attempt to answer the question if you can.

Think about starting your reply with one of these phrases.

- 'This is not something I know a lot about, but perhaps I could . . .'
- 'I have never been in this situation, but I imagine that . . .'
- 'I'm not sure about this, so I would check with a colleague/supervisor . . .'

However, if you really have no idea, then just be honest and say so. The interviewer may then explain the answer, or simply move on to the next question.

4. Questions that worry you

There may be a particular interview question that really concerns you and that you hope will not come up.

For example, you may have a gap on your CV, or be unsure how to explain your choice of qualifications or a low grade. Or perhaps you feel that you don't have enough work experience, or that it is not relevant enough.

If this is the case, make sure that you have really prepared for any questions that you are worried about. The temptation can be to avoid thinking about them, but in fact they are the ones to focus on first.

And when you are planning your answers, do remember that nobody is perfect. Your application has been good enough to get you an interview. So now you just have to work out the best way to deal with any awkward questions.

Dealing with questions that worry you

Example 1 Low grade

Explain that you were disappointed with that particular result – but that it did not reflect your real abilities and you are committed to working and studying hard.

Example 2 Work experience not relevant

Any work experience is always useful – so highlight any transferable skills that you gained such as time management, or teamworking skills.

Be honest in your answers, but also try to highlight any positive learning points. In this way you can show the interviewer that you have thought about the issue. You will also be more confident about dealing with any questions that arise.

Questions *you* can ask

There will usually be a chance for you to ask some questions at the end of your interview. A lot of people are not prepared for this opportunity. It is therefore worth planning some questions in advance because you want to aim for a good, positive end to your interview.

If you cannot think of any questions to ask, this might leave a negative final impression with the interviewer. It can make you appear uninterested and may leave the interview feeling rather flat.

So always prepare a couple of questions beforehand. Avoid asking anything about salary, holidays and any detailed contract issues. These are best left until you are actually offered the job. Instead focus on issues to do with the recruitment process and the job itself.

However, if all of your questions have been addressed during the interview, do explain this to the interviewer and thank them for covering all your queries.

Questions to ask

- When might I hear about the outcome of the interview?
- When will the job start?
- Will there be any introductory training?
- Who would I be working with?
- Which projects might I be involved with?

Before you leave your interview, always check when you should hear the outcome. There is nothing worse than wondering about this afterwards. Many interviewers will tell you, but if not, then do ask at the end of your interview.

How to practise interview questions

It is a really good idea to practise answering some interview questions beforehand. The aim is not to memorise answers word for word, as this will just sound stilted and false at your interview. And you will never be able to anticipate every question you will be asked, or predict an interviewer's questioning style.

Instead, begin by looking back through any information that you have about the job. Read your job application through carefully and make a note of any questions that you think might come up. Remember to include any questions that you are particularly concerned about.

Also think about the topics that you might be asked about – such as icebreaker questions, the job and the company.

Pick out some questions from the relevant parts of this chapter as well, and look at Chapter 10.

Then practise some individual questions in more depth by:

- writing down some notes about your answers
- practising out loud (by yourself, with a friend)
- having a mock interview with a careers adviser or interview coach.

Practising a few questions out loud can be particularly useful and trying this out by yourself will be very effective. And if you have enough time, get someone else to ask you a few questions as well.

This will help you to respond to questions more quickly and effectively.

Next steps

Even spending a short amount of time thinking about interview questions can be really useful. It can help to develop your confidence about answering a variety questions and ensure that you have relevant examples of your skills and experiences to highlight at the interview.

It can also help you to give more focused and relevant answers. This will help the interviewer to quickly understand important information about you. Additionally, it will highlight why you are best suited to the job.

It can also be useful to think through in detail how to answer some common interview questions. The following chapter therefore highlights the Top 10 interview questions that you might come across and how to handle them.

Checklist: questions, questions and more questions!

✔

Understand different questioning techniques ☐

Identify topics you might be asked about ☐

Understand tricky questions and how to answer them ☐

Identify any questions that worry you ☐

Practise answering questions:

■ out loud ☐
■ with a friend, relation, careers adviser ☐

Draw up a list of questions to ask the interviewer ☐

---

10 TOP 10 INTERVIEW QUESTIONS

There are lots of different questions that you might be asked at your interview, so it is hard to predict exactly which questions might come up. However, some questions do arise more frequently than others and can therefore be worth preparing for.

This chapter highlights some of the most common interview questions. They might be asked in a variety of different ways, but the main focus of the question will be the same.

It can be helpful to prepare and practise some of these questions in more depth before your interview. This means working out how to structure your answers, preparing some replies and practising them out loud.

Each of the Top 10 questions identified here offers ideas about what to include in your answer. There are also examples of answers that will help you to prepare your own personal responses.

This chapter will:

- ■ highlight the Top 10 interview questions
- ■ explain how to structure your answers
- ■ give examples of answers
- ■ help you prepare your own answers.

The Top 10 questions

The previous chapter outlined a wide variety of questioning styles and topics.

However, many interviewers draw on some very similar questioning approaches. They will often have prepared a list of things to ask you about. And this is likely to include some of the more popular interview questions.

Top 10 interview questions

1. Tell me a bit about yourself.
2. Why did you choose to study this particular subject/ course?
3. Why do you want to work for us?
4. Why did you apply for this job?
5. How would you describe yourself?
6. How would your work experience help with doing this job?
7. What are your strengths/weaknesses?
8. What is your greatest achievement so far?
9. Where do you see yourself in a few years' time?
10. Tell me about your hobbies/interests.

Each of these questions is described in turn here, along with some examples of answers. Also think about and write down your own answers. This will help you to learn how to answer them in a structured and effective way.

1. Tell me a bit about yourself

On the face of it, this is a really easy question – after all, you know lots about yourself!

However, it is a very broad and open-ended question. So it can actually be very difficult to decide just where to start and how much information to provide.

The key is to stay focused and highlight a few key points that you want the interviewer to know about you. And try to keep anything you say as relevant as possible to the job.

Aim to talk for about a minute and be clear when you have finished giving your answer. Try to avoid stopping abruptly, or drifting to a vague finish. Instead, try ending with a positive statement such as. 'Those are some key points: is there anything else you would like to know about?'

What to include

- A bit about your background – e.g. in final year of school, college.
- What you are currently doing – e.g. looking for your first job.
- Any interesting information – e.g. relevant work experience, interests, or key achievements.
- Your hopes and aspirations – e.g. prepared to study for further qualifications.

Example answer

I am in my final year at school where I am studying for my A levels. I am interested in becoming an accounting technician, so I am currently applying for training posts. I spent a week last year working in the accountancy department of a local company. I really enjoyed learning about different aspects of accountancy procedures. I also found out from the staff there about training as an accountancy technician and I'm prepared to work and study hard to pass all the relevant exams.

2. Why did you choose to study this particular subject/course?

An interviewer may ask you to talk about a course that you have chosen to study, or to explain why you did a particular combination of subjects. This is also an opportunity to describe to the interviewer what you have learned from your studies.

As this is another open-ended question, you also need to think about the structure and focus of your answer. So think about what information about your studies to include and the order in which to present it.

What to include

- What interested you about the course – e.g. key topics, structure, location.
- What you have learned – e.g. subject knowledge, special projects, practical tasks.
- Any key skills gained – e.g. communication, teamworking, time management skills.
- How all this relates to the job – e.g. key subject skills, practical skills.

Example answer

I decided to do a degree in biochemistry because I loved studying science at school. I particularly liked understanding how the human body works. During my degree course I also became very interested in medical processes, so I decided to do a research project about how cancer cells develop. As part of my course I also spent some time working in a hospital laboratory. I helped to set up and monitor some tests and experiments and enjoyed being part of such a knowledgeable team. As a result I am applying for a variety of scientific roles both within the NHS and with pharmaceutical companies.

3. Why do you want to work for us?

This can be a difficult question to answer if you do not know much about the company. Doing some research beforehand will therefore ensure that you can give an informed answer.

Most companies have a website, so always take a look at this before your interview.

If possible give some specific reasons that show your knowledge of the company, or the wider sector. This question can also be an opportunity to highlight which skills and personal qualities you could bring to the company.

What to include

- Short overview of any research that you have done – e.g. website, company brochure.
- Positive facts about the company – e.g. variety of clients, great products/service, training opportunities.
- Why you would be suited to the company – e.g. hard working, creative, customer focused.

Example answer

I was really impressed with your company website and the variety of IT systems that your training scheme would cover. As I am just starting my career, I would like to gain as much experience as possible. So I would really welcome the opportunity to be involved with supporting a range of IT projects. I am also hard working and like a challenge, so I would enjoy trying to solve different technical problems for staff as quickly as possible.

4. Why did you apply for this job?

With this sort of question, the interviewer really wants to find out if you understand what the job is about. They may also want to know why you are considering this particular type of work.

So this is an opportunity to highlight how your skills match what the company is looking for. Remember to draw on any relevant qualifications, work experience or hobbies that might help to support your interest.

What to include

- What aspects of the job interest you – e.g. working outdoors, meeting customers.
- Your key skills – e.g. administrative skills, IT skills.
- Any relevant work experience – e.g. Saturday job, work experience scheme.

Example answer

I would like to work as a receptionist because I really enjoy meeting people. I particularly understand the importance of representing the company and ensuring that customers feel welcome when they first arrive. When I did some office work experience with another local company last year, I worked on their reception desk for a day. I helped to greet people and check who their appointment was with. This was my favourite part of the work placement and what has led me to apply for this particular job.

5. How would you describe yourself?

This open-ended question requires you to identify some personal qualities and key skills. It is an important one to plan for, because a good answer will identify characteristics that are required for the job.

So check back to any details that you have about the job and see if these highlight any required qualities and skills. Also see Chapter 7 for help with identifying your own personal qualities and key skills. Try to give examples of when you have developed or used any personal qualities and skills. This will help to illustrate and support your description of yourself.

What to include

- Relevant personal qualities – e.g. quick learner, hard working, flexible.
- Skills that are relevant to the job – e.g. good communicator, problem solver, team player.
- Examples of these – e.g. relating to your studies, work experience, or hobbies.

Example answer

I am a very sociable and outgoing person, which is why I think I would make a good sales representative. I would enjoy going out and meeting clients and the challenge of winning new customers. I am also very organised and always willing to work hard to get a job done successfully. For example, last year I helped to get donations from companies for our Christmas fair at school. A group of us contacted local companies to ask them to give raffle prizes. I contacted the most companies and succeeded in getting three valuable donations as a result.

6. How would your work experience help with doing this job?

You may have done some work experience that is similar to the job you have applied for. Even if it is not directly related, you should always highlight any *transferable skills* that you gained.

Remember to be positive about your work experience as well. So do not say that it was badly organised or not relevant. Instead, emphasise what you learnt from the experience and the skills that you developed.

What to include

- What job you did and where – e.g. waitress in a local café, reception duties in a sports centre.
- Relevant key tasks – e.g. answering the telephone, dealing with customers.
- Transferable skills – e.g. communication skills, team working, time management.

Example answer

For my work experience I spent two weeks at a travel agency. I did a variety of tasks including filing, taking telephone messages and helping to book holidays for customers on the computer. A lot of the things that I learned there would be very useful in working as a sales assistant in your store. For example, I found out how important it is to be customer-focused – to be polite, listen carefully to the customer and help them find what they are looking for. I also understand the value of knowing about the products that you are selling in order to advise customers effectively.

7. What are your strengths/weaknesses?

You may be asked about either your strengths, or your weaknesses – and sometimes both. Most people find it much easier to identify some key strengths. This is because talking about weaknesses can potentially lead to focusing on negative issues.

What to include

Strengths

As with any questions about the sort of person that you are, try to highlight strengths that relate to the job. Also be prepared to give examples of occasions where you have displayed these strengths.

For example:

- good time manager
- get on with people
- work well under pressure.

Weaknesses

Identifying any weaknesses requires some careful thought. A good answer will try to turn the question around by highlighting a weakness that:

- you have overcome – e.g. impatient to get on with a new project, but have learned to plan carefully first
- could in fact also be a strength – e.g. rather a perfectionist, so like a job to be done well.

Example answers

I think my key strength is my ability to see a task through. I don't let a problem put me off and will always try to find a solution to make sure that a job is done on time.

My main weakness is that I am a bit of a perfectionist, so I like a job to be done really well. I do appreciate, though, the need to recognise when a project has been completed to a sufficiently high standard and then move on to the next task.

8. What is your greatest achievement so far?

This question requires you to talk about something that you have done which was useful, challenging or interesting. This could be anything from a fundraising project, gap year or sporting/music achievement.

Your answer should also highlight any skills that you used or developed. And if possible, these should be relevant to the job that you have applied for.

What to include

- A personal achievement – e.g. to do with your studies, work experience or interests.
- A recent achievement – e.g. within the last year or two.
- Some key skills – e.g. taking the initiative, team working, leadership.

Example answer

Last year I took part in a business competition at our school. There were several teams and each had to develop and present a business idea. Our team was selected to represent our school in a regional competition. We came third in that event and we were all really proud to have made it that far. I also learned a lot about how to develop a business plan and give a presentation to other people. It was good to work as part of a team as everyone had different ideas and skills. I was responsible for thinking about the marketing of our product and I enjoyed researching and planning our marketing strategy.

9. Where do you see yourself in a few years' time?

An interviewer is going to want to know that you plan to stay with the company for a reasonable length of time. They will also want to see whether your career goals fit with the company.

So with this type of question you want to demonstrate that you have thought ahead about your career plans. You also want to show that you are committed to working with this particular company.

What to include

- Key job achievements – e.g. develop key skills, work more independently.
- Completion of any training/qualifications – e.g. Apprenticeship, professional qualification.
- Taking on more responsibility – e.g. team leadership, project management.
- Gaining some wider experience – e.g. across the organisation, further training.

Example answer

My main priority would be to successfully complete my plumbing Apprenticeship. At that stage I would then look forward to working more independently. So I would enjoy visiting customers by myself and taking on the responsibility of diagnosing problems and resolving them. I would also be interested in understanding how to cost out jobs and prepare quotes for customers. This would give me a better understanding of how the business works and enable me to help the company to win new customers.

10. Tell me about your hobbies/interests

This question gives you the opportunity to talk more broadly about life beyond your study and work commitments. You may also have provided some information about your hobbies in your job application that the interviewer could pick up on.

Avoid any general topics, such as watching television, that are part of most people's routines. Instead, select one or two specific interests to talk about in more detail. And highlight any key achievements and skills that you have learned through a hobby.

What to include

- Give a brief overview of your key hobbies/interests.
- Describe the most interesting/relevant one – e.g. how long, key achievements.
- Explain what you have learned – e.g. key skills that you have developed.

Example answer

I am a big football fan and have played for my local team for the past eight years. It is great being part of the team and I love the challenge of playing in regular league matches. Last year we were asked if anybody would help to coach a junior team at our local school. I volunteered and have helped out since on a weekly basis. This responsibility has helped a lot to develop my leadership skills. It has also been really rewarding to see the team's football skills develop as a result and I am proud that they are doing well in their junior league.

Next steps

It can be very useful to think about how to answer some of the more popular interview questions. This means that you will be well prepared if these questions come up. It will also help you to become more skilled generally at providing focused and effective answers at your interview.

And if your interview is imminent, practising answers to the Top 10 interview questions will also be a good use of your preparation time.

As well as thinking about and writing out some answers, also remember to practise some of them out loud. This will get you used to the sound of your own voice and help to ensure that you keep your answers concise and informative.

Checklist: top 10 interview questions

✓

Read about the Top 10 interview questions ☐

Understand how to structure your answers ☐

Prepare your own detailed answers ☐

Practise answering questions:

■ out loud ☐
■ with a friend, relation, career coach ☐

---

11 WAITING TO HEAR . . .

You can focus a lot of time and energy on preparing for your first interview. Then suddenly the interview itself is over almost before you know it and you are left waiting to hear about the outcome.

This wait may take a day, a week, or sometimes longer. Even a day can seem like a very long time when you are wondering how you have done. It can also feel as though there is very little that you can do at this stage except wait.

It is possible to make some very good use of this time, though. It can be helpful to reflect on how your interview went and to write up some short notes about the experience. You also need to have a plan to keep busy and to decide what to do if the company does not contact you.

This chapter will:

- ■ help you review your interview
- ■ describe how to write up effective notes
- ■ identify strategies for managing the 'waiting game'
- ■ explain what to do if nobody contacts you.

Reviewing your interview

Prior to your interview, your thoughts are likely to have focused on the event itself. However, it is also worth having a plan to manage the time afterwards – while you are waiting to hear about the outcome.

Even if you feel your interview has gone well, this 'waiting game' can feel quite stressful. So it can be helpful to consider how to use this time to good effect. And it can be particularly useful to review how your interview went whilst it is fresh in your mind.

Your plan should cover three key stages once your interview is over.

1. Immediately after the interview.
2. Waiting to hear.
3. If nobody contacts you.

1. Immediately after the interview

Many people find that their interview seems to go surprisingly quickly. After all the planning and preparation, your interview is suddenly over and you are heading back home.

You might find yourself experiencing a whole range of different emotions immediately afterwards.

For example, you may feel:

- relieved that you have survived the experience
- pleased with the way that things went
- very tired if it has been a long day
- upset if you feel that the interview didn't go well
- anxious to know if you have got the job.

It is also very common to find yourself replaying the interview in your mind afterwards. Also to wonder how you did and if you will be offered the job as a result.

TIP It is difficult to know how you will feel after your interview, so arrange to call someone and let them know how it went.

You may therefore find it quite difficult to concentrate on anything for a while immediately after the interview, so it can be a good idea to set aside some time at this stage for reflection. This could be while you travel home, or perhaps by having something to drink and/or eat afterwards.

Some people also find it useful to speak to a friend, relation or colleague straight after their interview. Sharing the experience like this can be very helpful. It can also help you to calm down afterwards and get everything back into perspective.

2. Waiting to hear

Once your interview is over, you will also need a longer-term plan. You may hear from the company by the end of the same day, or it could take several weeks. This will all depend on the individual company and its recruitment process.

However long you have to wait, there are a lot of practical things that you can do, including:

- ensuring that you are contactable
- writing up some notes
- keeping busy
- continuing job hunting.

Ensure that you are contactable

The company should have advised you about when and how you will hear the outcome of the interview process.

Usually the successful candidate will receive a telephone call. This is generally the quickest way of contacting somebody and ensuring that they know the outcome. It also enables the company to check if the person is likely to accept the job.

So you clearly need to make sure that the company has the correct contact details for you. You may have provided a landline number, a mobile number, or both.

Telephone tips

- Keep your mobile telephone to hand.
- Ensure your landline number is accessible.
- Check telephone messages regularly.
- Keep your telephone fully charged.
- Avoid being out of contact for any lengthy period of time.

The likelihood is that you will jump every time the telephone rings. You will also probably find yourself checking for messages every few minutes to begin with. If you do happen to miss that vital call, however, the company will certainly make several attempts to contact you.

Write up some notes

It can be very useful to write up some notes about the interview. This can help you to get some perspective on how it went, and also to learn more effectively from the experience.

And just occasionally you may be asked back for a further interview. It can then be very helpful to have a record of what your original interview covered.

You do not need to write up pages of notes. Instead aim to capture the main points from your interview. Make a note of:

- names and job titles of people you met
- main areas of questions/answers
- any difficult questions/situations
- key information you learned about the job/company
- answers to any questions you asked.

These notes can be a really useful record if you ever have another interview. This process can also help to flag up any aspects of interview skills that you may need to work on.

Keep busy

After your interview, there can be a temptation to hover by the telephone. And this waiting stage can feel very lengthy and sometimes stressful. So it is worth having a plan that will help you to stay positive and make good use of the time.

In particular, try not to spend too much time dwelling on anything that you feel went wrong. People are often quite critical of their own interview performance. However, it is actually very difficult to know how you did relative to the other candidates on the day.

So do aim instead to keep reasonably busy and occupied. This can help to distract you and reduce your stress levels. It will also help the time to pass more quickly.

Top tips for keeping busy

- Keep to your usual routines of study or work.
- Meet up with friends.
- Do some exercise.
- Focus on a hobby/interest.

And if any aspect of your interview continues to worry you afterwards, do talk to someone about it. This could be somebody you know well, or a careers adviser. It can help a lot to share any concerns after your interview and to get them into perspective.

Continue job hunting

Until you have actually been offered a job, do keep looking for and applying for other work. This way you have a back-up plan if you are not successful in getting the job after your interview.

If you pin all your hopes on one particular interview, it can be particularly hard waiting to hear if you have got the job. Having some alternative applications under way can therefore really help to distract you and keep you busy.

3. What if nobody contacts you?

Some companies will let you know very quickly about the outcome of your job interview. Usually they will telephone the successful candidate and then follow up with an offer letter.

They may also telephone the remaining candidates to advise them that they have not been appointed. Alternatively they may write to let them know. And occasionally they will not contact unsuccessful candidates at all.

So this is why it is critical to know how the company plans to manage this process. If a clear deadline for hearing by telephone has passed, then it is unlikely that you have been successful.

However, occasionally an unexpected delay may arise in contacting candidates.

For example:

- the company may be waiting for a candidate to confirm if they will take the job
- the interview panel may have been unable to make a quick decision
- a candidate's references may not be satisfactory.

So if you do not receive a phone call or letter by an agreed date, it is quite acceptable to contact the company. If you have a named contact, telephone or email them. Otherwise telephone the company and ask the receptionist who you should speak to.

Next steps

The waiting period after your interview can feel very long and rather stressful. So it is important to have a plan for this stage and to make good use of the time. Clearly you need to be contactable if you are awaiting a telephone call, but it is also good to keep busy with other tasks.

It can be particularly helpful to take some time to reflect on how your interview went. Taking the time to write a few notes can be invaluable. This can help to get things in perspective and also enable you to learn from the experience.

Checklist: waiting to hear

	✔
Set aside some quiet time to reflect on your interview	☐
Ensure that you are contactable	☐
Write up some notes about the interview	☐
Have a plan to keep busy	☐
Continue job hunting	☐
Contact the company if you hear nothing by agreed date	☐

12 HOW TO HANDLE BEING OFFERED THE JOB, OR NOT

Once your interview is over, you may be very happy about how it went. Alternatively you might feel that there were some aspects that you could have improved on.

However you feel afterwards, it can actually be very difficult to judge whether you will be offered the job. The interviewer will take a wide variety of issues into account. And their decision will also depend on the range of other candidates being interviewed.

It is therefore worth planning for either possible outcome – being offered the job, or not. Clearly your aim in attending an interview is to convince the company to appoint you. And then you need to be prepared to manage a subsequent job offer professionally.

However, it can also be helpful to have a back-up plan if you are not successful. This will ensure that you learn everything you can from your interview experience. It will also help you to move on in a positive frame of mind with your job hunting.

This chapter will:

- explain what to do if you are not offered the job
- identify strategies for moving on
- describe how to manage a job offer professionally
- highlight which key aspects of your appointment to check
- offer tips for negotiating a deal.

If you are not offered the job

When you have spent a lot of time and emotional energy attending an interview, it can be *very* hard to learn that the job has been offered to someone else.

The reality with interviews, however, is that there are usually several candidates and only one job. You will therefore not be the only person to be disappointed. But this may not be much comfort if it was a job that you really wanted.

TIP Give yourself some time to deal with not being offered the job – and then plan a strategy for moving on.

It is therefore quite understandable to feel very disappointed when you hear the outcome. It might seem a real blow when you first find out – but it will be easier to come to terms with the news after a day or two.

There are also several useful and important things that you need to do.

- Contact the company to ask for some feedback.
- Write a thank you letter.
- Plan a strategy for moving on.

1. Contact the company to ask for some feedback

It can be very helpful to take some steps to find out why you did not get the job. It is therefore always worth contacting the company to see if they will give you some feedback.

This might seem really daunting, but it can help you to:

- take some practical action
- deal with the disappointment

- learn from the experience
- move on.

There may be a variety of different reasons why someone else was selected. Knowing why you did not get the job can therefore help you to understand the outcome.

Three key reasons for not getting the job

1. Another candidate was better qualified.
2. Another candidate had more relevant work experience.
3. You may not have given your best interview performance.

You can never predict who else will apply for a job – and sometimes there simply is a better candidate than you on the interview day. Perhaps they had more work experience, for example, or a wider range of qualifications. Knowing this can be very helpful. For example, perhaps you might consider doing some voluntary work to get some more relevant experience.

And sometimes your interview performance will not quite match up to someone else on the day. The vital thing to remember is that the experience will not have been wasted. You will have learned a lot from your first interview that you can take forward with you.

Top tips for getting interview feedback

- Speak to the interviewer if possible.
- Think about what you want to ask before you phone.
- Write down what you are going to say.
- Have a pen and paper to take notes.
- Be prepared for someone to call you back if they are busy.

2. Write a thank you letter

Even if you are not offered the job, it is a very good idea to write to thank the company for the interview opportunity. This will confirm your ongoing interest in this type of work and commitment to the company. It could then count in your favour if another job ever comes up. Address the letter to whoever interviewed you and keep it fairly short and simple.

What to include in your letter

- Which job you applied for.
- The date of your interview.
- Thank the company for the interview opportunity.
- Ask them to consider you if another vacancy arises.

Your thank you letter might look something like this:

Dear ....

I recently attended an interview at your company on .... for the role of ....

I am writing to thank you for the interview opportunity. It was really interesting to meet you and to learn more about both the job and the company.

I was disappointed not to be successful on this occasion, but hope that there might be another opportunity to work for your company in the future.

I would therefore be very grateful if you would consider me if another similar vacancy ever arises.

Yours sincerely

....

3. Strategies for moving on

It is important not to dwell too much on what has happened, and it can be helpful to have a plan for moving on after your first interview experience.

It is particularly important to keep busy. So avoid sitting at home thinking and instead keep up your usual routines. Also see friends, do some exercise and continue job hunting. Applying for as many vacancies as possible will improve your chances of getting another interview.

If you find it difficult to get over your disappointment, do talk to someone about this. Even a short chat with a friend can help. Or talk to a careers adviser who will be able to help you to learn from the experience.

There will be other interviews and jobs ahead for you. And you will be much better placed now to succeed with your next applications and interviews.

Managing a job offer effectively

Being offered the job after your interview is a brilliant outcome. All your hard work has paid off and the company now wants you to come and work for them.

So when someone calls to offer you the job, it might be a simple matter of thanking them and accepting the job.

Certainly the company will want to know if you are likely to take the job. However, you also need to ensure that you are clear about the offer that you are accepting. So at this point there may also be some details to discuss.

If you are attending interviews with several companies, it is also possible that you might find yourself managing more than one job offer. And a job may, with hindsight, not be the right one for you. In these situations you would therefore need to think through how to turn a job offer down.

So you need to plan ahead for a variety of scenarios if you are offered a job. These include the following.

- Managing the initial telephone call.
- Negotiating the best deal.
- Handling more than one job offer.
- Rejecting a job offer.

1. Managing the initial telephone call

Most companies contact the successful interview candidate by telephone. This call may come at any time, however, so it is worth being prepared beforehand.

In particular, you need to handle the call in a professional manner. As well as offering you the job, the company will want to check if you are likely to take up the appointment. And at this stage there may be some discussion about important details such as your starting date or salary.

Top tips for managing the initial telephone call

1. Answer the telephone call professionally:
   - answer the call yourself if possible
   - give your full name
   - speak clearly.
2. Keep a pen and paper to hand:
   - avoid having to hunt around for these
   - have them with your telephone
   - make sure that your pen works.

3. Find a quiet place to talk:
   - ensure that you can hear the caller clearly
   - move to a quieter location if necessary
   - find a place to sit down if possible.
4. If you miss a call from the company:
   - listen carefully to any message
   - call back as soon as you can
   - use the contact details you have been given
   - ask to speak to your named contact.

It is also really useful to prepare a checklist of any queries that you might have about the job. Many job offers are straightforward and you will already have all the information you need. However, it can be important to raise any key questions at this initial offer stage.

A common query is about the salary you will be paid. There are other details about a job, however, that you might want to check.

- Confirming the start date.
- Checking what hours/days you will work.
- Asking about induction training.

You also need to raise these issues politely. So begin by thanking whoever contacts you for the job offer and confirm that you are interested in accepting. Then mention that you have a couple of queries and check if it would be convenient to discuss them at this stage.

You will often be able to sort out most queries during this initial telephone call. It may not, however, be possible to confirm everything immediately. You may also want some time to think about the job offer.

It is quite acceptable to ask for 24 hours to consider any offer. You may also need to speak to the company again for a more

Points to discuss

- Thank the person who is telephoning.
- Make it clear that you are interested in the job.
- Politely raise any queries that you have.
- Ask if it would be convenient to discuss them at this stage.
- Check if the details of the offer will be confirmed in writing.
- Request some time to think about the offer if necessary.

detailed negotiation. Alternatively, the company may have to go away and check out some of the details before getting back to you.

2. Negotiating a deal

A company will usually have set out the main details about a job in, for example, the job advertisement. You may also have received further information at the interview.

It is important to check all these details carefully, however, at the offer stage. Salary is often the main issue in people's minds. There may, however, be lots of other details to think about and make sure that you are clear about.

Working arrangements to check

- Starting date.
- Type of contract (temporary, permanent, trial period).
- Hours of work.
- Flexible working.
- Shift arrangements.
- Pay.

- Holidays.
- Sickness benefits.
- Pension.
- Training arrangements.
- Redundancy terms.

Not all of these details may be relevant to the job you have applied for. Your aim is simply to avoid committing to anything that you might regret later. So you need to very clear about the job offer and clarify some details at this stage if necessary.

In your delight at being offered the job, it can be very easy to simply agree with everything that the company is offering. Many people are also uncomfortable with the idea of negotiating about details.

Some things such as the type of contract, or hours of work, may *not* be negotiable. Others such as the starting date, or pay, may sometimes be open to discussion.

Points to research

- The average salary rate for this type of work.
- Details of other company packages, e.g. holiday allowance.
- Expectations in terms of, for example, qualifications.

The quickest way to find out information about what other companies are offering can be online at recruitment websites. Look at similar jobs and any information about the working arrangements and salary. The aim here is to be informed, but realistic, about what you might negotiate.

For example, a company may be very clear beforehand that it will pay a fixed hourly rate. This may therefore not be open to any negotiation when you are offered the job.

Alternatively, the job may have been advertised with:

■ a salary range – from £ . . . to £ . . .
■ a salary 'in the region of . . .'

In these circumstances it may be necessary to negotiate the exact salary that you will be paid. For example, perhaps you are particularly well qualified, or have some relevant experience. You can then explain this to support a case for a higher rate of pay.

TIP If you are going to negotiate, always do some research so that you know what other companies are offering for similar work.

In these situations, some negotiation is therefore quite common. However, you need to be prepared for these discussions. You also need to make sure that anything that you agree is confirmed in writing.

You may receive a short appointment letter, or a more detailed contract. This could even be several pages long, so do take time to read through everything carefully. You should only write back to accept the job once you are happy and clear about all the details.

3. Managing more than one job offer

If you have a lot of job applications and interviews under way, it is possible that you will find yourself having to choose between two different job offers. Alternatively, you might be offered one job while you are waiting to hear the outcome of another interview.

In this case it may be possible to ask for some time to consider which one to take. A company will not wait indefinitely, but may be prepared to give you a short period of time to decide. Up to a week, for example, might be acceptable. However, a company will want to be able to offer the job to another candidate if necessary. So do agree a time/date deadline for you to notify them of your decision.

Also take steps yourself to ensure that you make the best decision possible. For example:

- *if you are waiting to hear from another company* – contact them to see when you might hear from them
- *if you are unsure which job to take* – try writing down the pros and cons
- *if you still cannot decide* – talk to a friend, family or careers adviser.

4. Rejecting a job offer

If you decide that a job is not the right one for you, let the company know as soon as possible. Speak to the person who offered you the job and thank them for the opportunity to work for the company.

Explain clearly why you have taken this decision. For example, perhaps you were offered more money or better training opportunities elsewhere. This will help the company understand why you are turning their job offer down.

It is also a very good idea to write a letter afterwards to explain your decision. This can be especially important if there is a chance you may apply to that company again for a job in the future.

Next steps

It is always wise to have a back-up option if you don't get the job. This is just good planning and means that you are well prepared for every eventuality.

It can be tough to come to terms with not being offered a post. However, you will have learned a lot from the experience – which might just be enough to tip the balance in your favour at your next interview.

And if you are successful, then checking out the offer is vital. This will ensure that you understand and are happy about the job that you are now about to start.

Checklist: how to handle being offered the job, or not

                                                                    ✔

Be prepared for being offered the job, or not ☐

Ask for feedback if you are unscuccessful ☐

Write to the company to thank them for considering you ☐

Prepare a list of any queries, e.g. salary, start date ☐

Research salary rates, terms and conditions ☐

Check the details of a job offer carefully ☐

Ask for time to consider the offer if necessary ☐

13 NEXT TIME!

Congratulations – you have made it through your first interview! You may have been offered the job, or perhaps not on this occasion. Whatever the outcome, you will certainly have learned a great deal from the process. And this is just the starting point for developing your interview skills throughout your career.

However many interviews you attend in the future, every one will be different. So reflecting upon the experience each time can be very useful.

This will help you to identify any key learning points and highlight what went well. It will also enable you to pick up on any interview skills that you need to work on and improve. The best way to do this is to draw up an action plan to develop your interview skills in the future.

This chapter will:

- help you to review your interview
- identify what went well
- highlight interview skills that you need to work on
- identify any other career management issues
- explain how to develop an action plan.

Reviewing your interview

By now you will have had some time to reflect on your first interview. You will also know the outcome of that interview. So you may be about to start your new job, or perhaps you are embarking on some further job hunting.

This is a very useful stage to carry out a review of your interview experience.

You can reflect on:

- your own views about how the interview went
- any feedback you may have received from the company.

Whether or not you were offered the job, there are likely to be some things that went well at your interview. However, there may also be some aspects of the experience that you feel could have gone better.

The aim at any future interview is to build on what went well. It is also important to identify where you may need to work on your interview skills. You can then address these issues so that you are well prepared for any future interviews.

It can be useful to begin your review process by looking back at any notes that you took after your interview (see Chapter 11). If you asked for any feedback about your interview, take this into consideration too.

Then complete the following quiz. This will ask you to think about different aspects of your interview and how you felt they went.

---

20 Questions Quiz: how did my interview go?

	Yes	OK	Not really
1. Was I happy with my interview performance?	☐	☐	☐
2. Did I do enough preparation?	☐	☐	☐
3. Did I arrive on time?	☐	☐	☐
4. Was my interview outfit appropriate?	☐	☐	☐

	Yes	OK	Not really
5. Did I know enough about my job application?	☐	☐	☐
6. Did I know enough about the job?	☐	☐	☐
7. Did I know enough about the company?	☐	☐	☐
8. Did I cope with the interview format?	☐	☐	☐
9. Did I do myself credit in any selection tests?	☐	☐	☐
10. Was my presentation successful?	☐	☐	☐
11. Did I create a good first impression?	☐	☐	☐
12. Did I smile?	☐	☐	☐
13. Did my handshake work?	☐	☐	☐
14. Did I use positive body language?	☐	☐	☐
15. Did I answer all the questions?	☐	☐	☐
16. Did I give concise and focused answers?	☐	☐	☐
17. Did I ask some useful questions?	☐	☐	☐
18. Did I feel confident?	☐	☐	☐
19. Did I keep my nerves under control?	☐	☐	☐
20. Did I get across key information about myself?	☐	☐	☐

Identifying what went well

Any quiz questions where you answered 'Yes' are areas where your interview skills are already well developed. You can take these skills forward to any future interviews and feel confident that they will be effective.

If you did not answer many of the questions with a 'Yes,' don't worry. Becoming skilled at interviews takes time and practice. You have already shown that you can get yourself successfully to the interview stage. Now you just need to work on strengthening your interview skills further.

What interview skills do you need to work on?

Any quiz questions where you answered 'OK' or 'Not really' are areas where you need to do some more work on your interview skills. This is why it is so useful to do a review of your interview experience – you can now come up with a focused plan to improve your skills.

What do you need to work on?

Only one or two interview skills issues

Examples:

- you did not do enough research about the company
- you got stuck on one particular question
- your handshake was not very confident.

These are all very specific issues. A bit more research and preparation before your next interview will help you to address these. So make these issues a key priority when you are planning your preparation for another interview.

A key interview skills issue

Examples:

- you did not have enough time to prepare well enough
- you found it difficult to keep your nerves under control
- you found it hard to answer a lot of the questions.

It may be useful to start some work to address these issues straight away. Then you will have plenty of time to prepare and practise. You will also be ready even if an interview comes up at short notice next time.

You also need to think about how much more work you may need to do. It could just be a bit of extra preparation before your next interview. Alternatively, you may want to get working on some issues straight away – even before you have another interview scheduled.

Once you have identified the main areas of interview skills that you need to work on, you need to think about the steps to take to address them.

For example, you could:

- revisit the relevant chapter(s) in this book
- prepare interview answers for any questions you found tricky
- practise a wide variety of selection tests
- book some interview coaching.

Identifying other career management issues

Interviews can also prompt you to think more widely about your career plans. This is more likely to happen if you were not offered the job, or if you were offered the job, but realised that it was not the one for you.

There are three main issues that can arise.

1. You do not have any more interviews lined up.
2. You realise that you may need more qualifications or relevant work experience.
3. You wonder if this might not be the job/career for you.

So you may find yourself needing to improve your job hunting strategy, or reconsidering your career plans. If this happens it is worth giving some time and thought at this stage about how to go forward.

Top tips for career management

1. Improve your chances of getting interviews:
   - review your CV to make sure that it is up to date and effective
   - widen your job search including newspapers, recruitment agencies, online sources and personal contacts
   - increase the number of job applications you are making.
2. Improve your qualifications and work experience:
   - review your qualifications and consider whether you need to do any further study
   - do some voluntary work to gain more relevant work experience.
3. Review your career options:
   - research a variety of other career options
   - speak to a careers adviser.

Developing an action plan

Identifying the interview skills and career issues that you need to do some work on is useful, but you also require an effective plan to tackle them. This will ensure that you are fully prepared in good time for any future interviews.

A good way to achieve this is to do some action planning. This process includes identifying the steps that you need to take to improve your interview skills. It also involves deciding how long this is going to take and when you should aim to complete each task.

The idea is to draw up a practical and focused action plan. This will ensure that you actually get on and develop your interview skills further, rather than just thinking about it.

Your action plan

Step 1 Where am I now?

You have already reviewed how your interview went. So now write a list of the main things that you want to work on. These might be to do with your interview skills, or any other career management issues that you have identified.

Be specific about each of the issues that you are trying to address. This will help to keep your plan clear and relevant.

Example:

I answered some interview questions effectively, but a lot of my answers were too long and unfocused.

Step 2 Where do I want to be?

This is where you decide your goals – which means where you want to get to. Be as precise as possible about this as it will help you to focus on exactly what you want to achieve.

Example:

I want to be able to answer a variety of interview questions in a confident, focused and effective way.

Step 3 How do I get there?

This is where you set out the strategy that you will use to achieve your goal. It needs to include the steps you will need to take and when you aim to complete them.

Example:

- read through Chapter 9 'Questions,   Date: _____
  questions and more questions'

- read through Chapter 10   Date: _____
  'Top 10 interview questions'
- prepare draft answer to each   Date: _____
  Top 10 interview question
- practise my answers out loud   Date: _____
- book a mock interview with   Date: _____
  careers adviser.

Step 4 Taking action

Now you need to get on and put your plan into action. Tick off each step as you complete it and try and stick to your target dates.

You might have just one key action that you need to work on, or you may have several. And you might be able to complete your action plan in one day, one week, or one month. The timescale will depend on how much you are hoping to do and what is realistic for you to achieve.

Whatever your action plan looks like, you will be setting out to build on your interview skills for the future.

Next steps

The experience that you gain from your first interview is invaluable. It is only by actually going through the real thing that you begin to get an idea of how your interview skills are developing.

By reflecting on the experience afterwards, you can then begin to see what was effective. You can also identify any areas where you need to do some more work.

Drawing up an action plan to address these issues means that you will be able to ensure that you are ready for your next interview!

Checklist: next time!

	✔
Reflect on your interview and any feedback	☐
Complete the 20 Questions Quiz	☐
Review what went well at your interview	☐
Decide which interview skills you need to work on	☐
Identify any other career management issues	☐
Draw up an action plan	☐
Put your plan into practice	☐